Standing In God's Grace

WOMEN'S COMPILATION PROJECT

Volume 2

Featuring:

Nina Bailey-Fletcher
Dr. Cortesha Cowan
Toni R. Davis
Taril Gravely
Kimberlli Hollings
Carolyn House
Jill Howard
Cathey W. Law
L'Tarra Moore
ShaConda Nelson
Dr. Odunayo Obisesan, CPLC
Janet Phillips-Crawford
LaTanya Settles
Angel Tucker
Marilynn Walker

Published by
Again I Rise Publishing
Chicago, Illinois

Printed in the United States of America

ISBN: 978-0-9986148-1-6

Library of Congress Control Number: 2017941861

Cover and Interior Design by Jessica Tilles/TWA Solutions

All stories appear courtesy of the authors, unless otherwise noted.

Scriptures used are taken from the New King James Version Bible.

The Women's Compilation Project is hosted by Mutual Partners Association, which is nonprofit organization that implement after-school and summer programs for youth in urban communities. The proceeds from this book will help pay for youth to attend after-school and summer programs that teach character development, self-esteem, leadership skills and experiential learning through fun activities such as theater, music, art, dance and sports.

Acknowledgments

First and foremost, I would like to thank my Lord and Savior Jesus Christ for entrusting me with this project. Truly, without Him, none of this would have been possible. I would like to thank my mother, Mary Loretta Burns, for her love and support. You are an amazing woman who taught me to be a giver and to be loving and compassionate toward others. Mom, you have been my lifetime support system and I appreciate the love you show me daily. I love you with all my heart! I am very grateful to my husband, Abdoulaye Diarrassouba's, for his support, love, and daily encouragement. God truly blessed me the day we met. I would like to thank my late father, Leroy Tripplett, who always believed in me. Whenever I thought I could not do something, he would say, "Baby, you can do it." He was such a wonderful dad who taught me the philosophy of life and how to live life intentionally. I would like to thank my extended family as well for always supporting me in the many endeavors I have embarked upon; Lord knows I have done a few.

God has placed some of the most amazing people in my life. I would specifically like to thank all the women who have consistently supported The Experience Now® and The Girlfriend's Weekend Retreats. These women have been amazing and I truly consider all of them the sisters I never had. With deep gratitude, I would like to thank all the women who participated in The Women's Compilation Project. I do not take your participation lightly. You opened your hearts to this project and entrusted me throughout the process of creating this book. I know it's God's will and His divine order that we all have come together to contribute to something greater than ourselves. I am forever thankful for your obedience to God's call to participate in this project. I could not have done this without your loyalty and commitment.

In addition, I would like to thank my trusted mentor, Deborah Dillon, who inspired me many years ago to start my own business and in 2006, I made that dream a reality and started a nonprofit organization. I could not have done that without her guidance and motivation. Throughout the years, she has given me encouragement; I am thankful to have Deb in my life. Finally, I would be remiss not to mention my editor, Jessica Tilles, who worked tirelessly with me until we got this project just right.

Thank you all from the bottom of my heart.

Bridget Burns-Diarrassoba
Publisher

Table of Contents

≫ NINA BAILEY-FLETCHER ≪

The Precursor

The Precursor
A True Story

I was nineteen years old, trying to figure out how to begin a life in a world that was ending at Armageddon, which was to come soon. I was emotionally spent, heartbroken for the first time in my life, and although I had spent an entire lifetime studying and teaching scripture, I found myself trying to find my own spirit.

The road I was traveling seemed so long ahead, but too turbulent behind me to turnaround. I was exhausted from the weight of my own thoughts and convictions, some of which were programmed and some of which were earned as a result of decisions I'd made under that programming. Nonetheless, as my grandfather always told me, "Sweets, there is no way but forward and no direction but upward or onward."

You see, when you are at the crossroads of what has always been, and what is to come, there are two major challenges. First, assessing whether the way things have always been will be beneficial to you in the challenges that are to come. Second, approaching the things that are to come with an open sensibility and nonjudgement so as to have a clear and discerning mind to move forward. The first challenge is based on solutions to experiences in the past. The latter is based on skills that are raw and undeveloped. In my story, I have found that this is when your

Precursor will appear. When it is too hard to go back, and the only light going forward is the one inside of you.

This is a true story about the day my Precursor appeared. I am sharing the story so others, too, may identify their Precursor.

I found myself wandering in a local supermarket. I suppose everyone else had lighter things on their minds, but I had the weight of the world on my shoulders, it seemed. When people looked at me, they saw a beautiful face with a countenance that would scare a lion! My tolerance was nonexistent, and my male counterparts would run the other way. Nevertheless, I was determined I was going to get myself some steamed crabs legs so at least for the twenty minutes I reclined to eat them I would have some peace from my thoughts. And then it happened.

"Hello," he said.

I looked away and quickly ignored the handsome man in the dark blue work suit and work boots, short black afro and hat, complete with a radiant smile, clean cut, and well spoken, although he had only said one word. I guess you could tell from my accurate description of him how successful I was at ignoring him. Oh yes, and he was about five-foot-eleven, slender build with the most beautiful dark brown skin, and a goatee. Yup! I was really ignoring this dude! Anyhow, he continued moving closer to me.

"Hello," he spoke softly as he smiled and took a step.

I then swiftly unloaded my arsenal of defenses on him like it was yesterday's lunch and today's snack.

"Uh, look, boo, I am not looking for a boyfriend, just got rid of one. Not giving out my number, not good for any romantic conversation right now. Take a number and get in line. Better yet, take a seat...over there. Have a good one!" I replied crassly.

"I'm sorry, I didn't mean to upset you, but has anyone made you smile today? You are truly beautiful, and I know that on a normal day you have extended yourself to brighten the days of others. I know that you are blessed and deeply loved," he stated.

Just then, the patron in line behind me asked me to move up because there was no one in front of me. I turned around and virtually blazed his nostril hairs when I said, "I'm talking to someone!" The man's response was, "No one is there." I called him crazy and decided to move ahead so I could place my order and keep the peace.

"And how would you know that one? How would you know I was blessed and deeply loved?" I said sarcastically, returning to my original conversation with the handsome man with no name.

"Here is what I know. I know that you are looking for an answer. That answer is not an explanation or reasoning, it is more of a compass. You know well what your job is. But you are not developed in how to do it, and you look for a pattern but cannot find one. You are dealing with attacks and are not sure how to defend yourself. You endure the trauma because what you are and what you are carrying is more important than the pains enforced by the attacks. You do so every day, knowing that you will be taken care of and healed, even though you don't know what to do to stop the attacks." As he talked, he looked right through me as if to see something else than the body that stood in front of him.

"I'll continue," he said, "I know that you know scripture cover to cover. I know that it is in your heart, but you do not feel the love and compassion from God for yourself, that you teach others God has for them. You don't know how. You don't know why. Your heart is guarded…but not hardened, which is why you can hear me. It is also why you continue to love and to work."

Grabbing my crab legs quickly and feeling extremely naked at this point, I hid my face so as not to show the tears welling in my eyes. The truth was, I had just prayed over exactly those things before leaving my home that day. You see, I had been having literal arguments with God over my condition, my family, the lack of love, and finding a way out of my condition. I could not clearly see a way to complete what I knew I needed to. But I had not discussed this with anyone.

"I am not changing my religion, I already know Jesus…I already know God," I insisted.

He simply replied, "I never said you didn't know God. I never said God has not seen you. Also, your religion or what mine might have been is no longer relevant as this is a spirit conversation. Your understanding of the Bible is excellent and your belief is strong, but there is a KNOWING that you have left to discover that has nothing to do with religion."

I thought for a moment and replied, "For God is a Spirit and those worshiping him must worship him in spirit and in truth." At that point, my countenance softened, but my defenses were still at high alarm. "I can perceive this as truth, and we can have a conversation based upon this principle. You may continue."

Now, it helped his case that he was absolutely gorgeous and smiled a lot, but what kept me in the conversation was that he was in KNOWING of something that I knew not. I needed to know what exactly that was. I didn't say it to him, but he continued.

"Yes I can help you figure on what that is."

"What?" I asked, knowing clearly that I had not expressed my thoughts, but he had answered them.

"Religion is simply a language to express a spirit principle; you convey spirit meaning from what a person understands as the language of their religion. Do you understand what the Spiritual Coat of Armor is?"

"Yeah, Breastplate of Righteousness etcetera, etcetera," I replied. "Go on…"

He laughed and said, "Very good; you know what it is. What you don't know is where it is, how to activate it, and how to use it. Everyone is built with a spirit defense, and it has to be activated in order to protect you. You are aware that it exists, but your Journey will teach you to activate it. Open your ears, and soften your heart, God is tired of seeing you beat up through lack of Knowledge."

I did just as he asked. Throughout that conversation, the man answered questions I had only perceived in my mind and not vocalized with the utmost clarity. I truly mean I had not vocalized my true thoughts and he answered them as if they were stated clear as a sunny day in June. I lengthened my shopping trip just to spend extra time in his knowledge. The spiritual nature in which he communicated was more beautiful than his voice and his body, and believe me, that was really hard to do! He was absolutely beautiful.

Perhaps what is to follow is what absolutely brought me to my knees.

As we left the store, I was heading to my car, but decided to walk slowly because I did not want him to see my car and follow me.

He said, "Oh, don't worry. I'm not going to follow you to your car," and laughed at me. This was yet another thought I had not vocalized that he answered. "I almost hate to leave you, but I think you will be okay. Remember what you have been taught, and remember you are seen, you are loved, and you are blessed."

The parking lot was virtually empty and I have a habit of parking at the far end of the lot to walk for exercise. There was nothing but open space. I turned for five seconds to retrieve my keys from my pocket and motion to my car and then turned back. In an open parking lot, the man had disappeared. With no cars around and nowhere he could have gone. He should have been still standing there and he was gone. I only remember a stiff wind brushing through me as if I was an open window. As suddenly as he came, he was gone.

Now, up to this point at age nineteen, I had endured domestic abuse, paranormal experiences from unfriendly spirits, passive aggressive and emotional abuse, racism and the psychological wars that accompany it (that no one talks about), and a very devout and controlling religious life. Sometimes, we hide our pain behind our religion, making it very hard to heal our spirit through faith. But now I understood. There was a piece of my Spirit Being that no being or religion would ever own because I had been given the means to protect it.

Why was this man the Precursor? Because what I had to endure afterward was much more intense. Between the ages of nineteen and twenty-nine, I would again endure domestic abuse, but this time as a wife, racism, divorce and single motherhood, poverty conditions, disassociation for no cause, alienation, and a separation of my faith and spirituality from my religion, which is like tearing the soul from the body.

For every highest high moment, there was the lowest low, but I could not have done it without the conversation I had with that man that day.

You see, your Precursor will come when you have come too far to turn around, and there is no road map forward. That Precursor will come when you are most guarded, most confused, and most frustrated, but will leave you with the tools needed to fulfill your purpose.

Incidentally, I had a detailed argument with God approximately three years later. I was questioning His realness and whether He heard me, and inquired of His origins. I demanded a sign. I went to the Corner Market one morning and walking through those doors I heard that familiar voice, "Nina..."

Now let me be clear. I do not ever remember giving my name, but I knew that voice and in the same outfit with the same smile was the man.

"You look good! You are progressing on what you have been told. Be patient with yourself and your situation, it will take time," he said.

I grabbed his hands and he pulled me around the side of the building to shield me from the wind as it was a cold winter day.

I don't remember what I said from that point because I knew I was dealing with something much bigger than myself. All I remember was asking for his name. His name was Alan. He then said he needed to get back to work and that I would be okay and to keep going. I reluctantly released his hands because I knew when he turned the corner he would be gone. And no less than three seconds later, just like before, he was gone with only the same stiff breeze to go through me like an open window.

Nina Bailey-Fletcher is an accomplished singer, songwriter, and producer. She has recorded on two publically released CDs, the second of which is her debut CD *Nina Fletcher, Courage* released in 2009. Her debut earned a 3 ½ out of 5 star review from Karl Stark of the *Philadelphia Daily News* and continues to receive recognition. She has performed at many of the major jazz festivals and jazz houses on the East Coast, and continues in her work in many ways.

Nina Bailey-Fletcher

Nina invests her time in co-producing music shows in the Tri-state area, conducting public speaking engagements, and performing for a mixed audience of men and women of all ages. Her charitable works include being a VIP Member of the National Association of Professional Women in 2015, and a self-created grass roots effort entitled "12 Things New To You," an effort to encourage career women in maintaining a healthy lifestyle by incorporating whole foods and fresh fruits and vegetables into their busy routines. Nina hopes to release her next project in 2018 entitled *The Ballad of Nine, Nina Fletcher*. We are in eager expectation of great things to come.

≫ DR. CORTESHA COWAN ≪

Pushed Myself Into Leadership

Pushed Myself Into Leadership

Part 1

I am Dr. Cortesha Cowan. I approach each task with boldness and determined to reach my destination despite any obstacles and challenges that come my way. As a woman with strength, I try my best to inspire others to discover their passion plan and purpose to pursue their dreams. I have always been one to encourage them to PUSH. We all are born mighty warriors. Based on Philippians 4:13, it tells us *"I can do all things through Christ who strengthens me,"* so in this chapter, I am going to talk about how many times God has allowed me to hit the reset button because He was and is not done with me yet. I will walk you through my story. How I had to go deep in the word of God, to renew, refresh and restore my faith in the things He wanted me to do and to also take me to my next journey…my best journey. It is said in the world, "When you fall, you get back up and try again." I have done just that, over and over, time and time again.

I PUSH myself to keep going because I have my three children watching and they need to see what "getting back up" look like. I have always PUSHed past my fears. So can you. In

2008, I had to PUSH again as I was on a path that would lead to my owning and becoming the Founder and CEO of Mothers Helping Mothers in Columbus, Ohio. A non-profit that helps teen mothers and their babies get on track toward a better life. I was born and raised in Lima, Ohio where about the age of eight, I started to take care of my little sister, cousins and even much older cousins. Seemed a little crazy because I had two older cousins who in turn looked up to me when I felt it should be the other way around. I have a heart for helping others because every time I saw that someone was in need I kept trying to help fix it. I knew that I would be in a generation filled with leaders so I started very early. Most of my friends help others to. And today as adults most of us are giving back. I have always been a leader, never seeing myself as a follower. I knew I had a purpose to do something big in my life. I was just trying to figure out what the purpose was, but I knew it was helping people, I just felt it. Was I making myself be different from others right from the beginning? Standing out by always helping a teacher, neighbor, or friend, and of course, I couldn't leave family out. My grandmother taught me the value of that. Because of my strong desire to help my grandmother, I learned so much from her. For her, the importance of family was everything. So I spent as much time as I could around her. I remember going from family to family, helping her clean their homes, and getting us ready for the week for school. When it comes to learning how to survive and serve others, my grandmother played such a big part in my life. However, after her death in 1993, I never knew learning how to serve others was about to get real for me. Survival and serving became a typical part of my life.

Trusting myself and knowing the survival skills I have learned from my grandmother, anything that came my way I knew how to handle it. I started to use it more often than I wanted. After January 1993, it got very hard for me after the passing of my grandmother. At that time, both my mother and father were in jail. The family member that came to live in my mother's home with us was really not on track. I had to learn the hard way of surviving with my little sister. I know it's hard for my mother to believe, but her going away for thirteen months taught me to grow up a lot faster than she would like to think. Not in the way of having sex, going out, doing drugs, or anything of that sort, it was more so learning how to take care of myself, my little sister and little cousin who also stayed with us. This time in my life was when I really started to learn how to grow and advocate for my family members younger than me. God released and equipped me with such a task that would also teach me in the near future how to embrace and impact others around me in such a good way. I had to learn how to feed us because the family member that lived with us wasn't always there. However, we never went without eating, not on my watch. We never went without clean clothes on our back for school, not on my watch. The family members responsible for us weren't there like they should have been. Instead, they spent time fighting each other. Due to the lack of support for us, by age fourteen, I was doing it all. I discussed our living situation often with my mother when she would call. Although, we didn't get to talk every day because it was hard keeping a phone in the home, updating her took place in a span of a twenty-minute phone call.

I would pray to God to give me the tools and PUSH I needed to overcome this brokenness at this stage in my life. I had to start being the mommy for my younger family members, because I already carried the name "Tishamommy" that the family gave me so early in life. I started to believe it, and I was empowered to move forward. Caring for others became so easy to me, so the rest of my childhood and even after my mother came home, I played a big role as "Tishamommy". All of this is to say there's not an age that God cannot equip you to stay on track and to do the right things.

Part 2
"Tishamommy" grown for real now!

Yes. I was all grown now. I was about to overcome being a teen mother. I gave birth to my son at the age of sixteen. I was not like most girls my age. Caring for a baby was not new to me. I had to care for my little sister and other family members at such an early age, but having my own child made me grow even faster. I was a natural caretaker. As a young black woman, I had to care for my son, doing the best I could to keep him from being around things that could not be good for him; I made sure that falling on my face as a teen mother was not an option. By working a job and staying in school, I knew that one day he was going to need more, so I was always going above and beyond to provide excellent parenting care for him. I have very strong values about how I wanted my life to be for my son and me. I realized and understood the responsibilities that came with being a young mother. I kept doing the best for him; having the best for him was my ultimate goal and making smart moves that would benefit us. I remained very humble as a child growing up; I knew I could face anything and still take it as if it didn't bother me. I never expected it would happen again my last year of high school. I was nineteen years old when I was about to have my baby girl. What was I to do with two kids now on my last year in high school? My PUSH got stronger. My first responsibility was the wellness and safety of my two children.

At that time, I decided to take a leap of faith with my boyfriend, who is now my husband. We moved to a bigger place. We moved to where we could financially get in a better position, where we could get away from so much negativity, and where we could become stronger partners to raise our children. Moving to Columbus, Ohio in 2000 changed my life for the better, leaving the lack of focus back home. I left behind my trying to keep up with what everyone was doing and also became the bigger person on so many personal issues that I was having with others. I left behind trying to play mommy to so many while I had my own babies. Leaving Lima was the best thing I could have done. I had to remove myself and my family away from the many people that were either trying to take advantage and some that just wanted to stay in the same place they were in. I knew it wasn't for me and I knew it wasn't a place that I can raise my children. Once I got settled as a teacher here in Columbus, my eyes started to open to what giving really looked like. I was determined to achieve my goals and change my life after working for a while as a teacher in a childcare center. I prayed and asked God what was my next move. Things were going so good. Then, my grandfather passed. Now I know I moved away, but I still talked to him on the phone and saw them all when I could. At least, I got the chance to ask him, "Granddaddy, why did you start your own business?"

"Baby, start one to leave something for your children not one just to make money," he said. "Do something that will last more than just in your life and theirs."

I knew right then my true purpose started to cook inside of me. I was known as "Tishamommy" in Lima, Ohio, but God was about to rename me, and I had no idea.

Part 3

I will become a well-respected and sought after fixture within our communities. I was not ready for that purpose and responsibility that God was placing on my life, but in 2008, it happened. I was entrusted with building a model for teen mothers and their babies that were homeless or lacked support. These teen mothers needed to get back on track. I became an active member of the community and I became engaged in building the teens and young girls back up. By 2011, I was also working to do the same for young women ages eighteen to twenty-five. No one could stop this; I had to keep saying, "I am a revisionary that knows what God has for me and what I'm sought out to do in this world." Also saying this over and over, "I will become an extraordinary history-maker who will keep empowering and transforming the lives of teen mothers and young girls." In 2015, God said to me and my business partner, as clear as day, "Now adults, children, and seniors in your area." All I could think at this point was, God, You know how much I can handle and what I can do.

This was definitely possible, as I was a teen mother that overcame many obstacles. Thinking and pushing myself made me such a great mentor and advocate for teen moms. For the rest of the community, I have been to several training sessions, I have owned a few childcare facilities, learning the development of their well-being, and how they grow and think. As for seniors, my business partner helped to bring that back to my life. Back home in Lima, I used to work in senior care programs and at the hospital, but it was rebirthed after I met my business partner. I received numerous awards and accolades that got me to the next level, and I received my Doctorate Honorable Degree along with so many other things. On January 21, 2017, I received The

Presidential Lifetime Achievement Award from President Barack Obama.

When you PUSH yourself, things happen. I am set up to help others find their purpose in this life. I hope this has helped you understand that no matter where you came from or who you came from, know that God created you first and He knows what's best. He knows what you can and cannot handle. He knows what you are going to go through and how you are going to come out. As long as you remember those things, you can conquer this world. Keep peace of mind, knowing that God allows things to happen, and it is so worth what the outcome will be. Never did I think that this young teen mom from Lima, Ohio would own a center for teen moms, a childcare center, play a big role in a home health agency, receive an honorable doctorate degree, be in two books, and receive such a high award all the way from the White House…but God. PUSH and sow seeds and the doors of heaven will send down blessings. Have integrity and try to make smart investments that will benefit the world as a whole. This journey has not been easy, or paved. I have had to work hard to get where I am today. And there is so much more I still have to do.

"I can do all things through
Christ who gives me strength,"
– Philippians 4:13

Dr. Cortesha Cowan is the Founder/ CEO of Mothers Helping Mothers Inc. She was a teen mom who grew up in Lima, Ohio. With the support of her family and her innate drive to succeed, she maintained school attendance, activities, and employment until graduation. Upon moving to Columbus, Ohio, she became a childcare teacher and currently owns a childcare center called Cozy Corner Home of Care & Love LLC. She is known as "The Confidence Coach" for her ability to help women and young girls grow their confidence and passion for what they are trying to do. She is a straightforward coach that develops the passion in women and young girls.

As a female-entrepreneur, Dr. Cowan has worked hard to build a step-by-step system and amazing model for opening homes for teen and young mothers that are homeless and in need of support services. She has leveraged her professional and personal experience to empower and help teen mothers, young girls and women grow.

Dr. Cowan's main goal in life is to educate, empower, and support others. In 2008, God gave her the vision to help teen mothers to become self-sufficient by being a resource to young mothers and their children. This vision expanded to providing safe shelter at the Haven of Hope crisis and transitional house and empowerment through programs at MHM and local partner organizations.

Dr. Cowan has been nominated and awarded for countless awards, including the 2013 International Women's Day recognition award and was nominated by Kaplan University for the Community Service Alumni award in 2013, which was presented by the Ohio Association of Colleges and Schools. Other recognition included Community Service Award 2013 from Youth for Positive Image, 2013 Outstanding Community Service from national Council Of Nero Women, Micro Entrepreneur of the year Award 2015, Honorary Doctorate Degree 2015, nominated for the NAACP Hometown Champion 2015, Nominated for Woman of the Year 2015 at Faith Life Church, Nominated for female-entrepreneur Global 2016, nominated, honored and awarded Excellence in Leadership for teen mother support 2016 and also holds a Certification in Life Coach and Christian Life Coach.

In January 2017, Dr. Cowan was awarded The Presidential Lifetime Achievement Award from 44th President Barack Obama, and she now holds the title of Global Ambassador for The Unstoppable Woman Of Purpose Global Movement.

Dr. Cowan The Confidence Coach
www.DRCORTESHACOWAN.com

※ TONI R. DAVIS ※

Are You Ready?

Are You Ready?

Are you ready?

No.

Are you ready for the journey–for I have much work for you to do?

No.

Am I ready?

No. Who said that? My heart? My head? My flesh? No!

Wait…Wait…

What if, Lord…You said You wouldn't leave nor forsake…I'm just so afraid.

You see, what if I don't sing right?

What if I don't witness right?

What if the way I dress…well, they don't like the way I dress.

What if…what if…what if?

Trust me.

What if…

Trust me.

But what if sista-so-and-so don't like me?

What if brotha-know-it-all can't handle the word coming from someone like me?

What if Mrs. Know-it-all, who does it all, done it all, volunteers for it all and knows how it's always been done, and how it's going to be done...her looks can be poisonous.

Trust Me, child.

What if my child is too loud in church?

What if my husband says he don't want me spending time at church?

What if...What if? What if?

Trust Me, child.

Stand on My faith.

Walk in My shadow.

Rest in the shade of My tree for it has many branches.

Sit at My banquet table for you will never know hunger.

Drink from My well and the cooling waters of knowledge will sustain you.

But my past, Lord, my past. Some people won't let you forget.

I forgive you.

Take My hand child and let Me lead you.

Yes. Lord. yes.

Are you ready?

Are you ready for the journey I am about to take you on?

26

Are You Ready?

I am a woman of God who has been abundantly blessed by His compassion and forgiveness. I am a woman of God who continues to be amazed by God's awesomeness. I am a woman of God who has come to the realization that without The Lord in my life, I could not be a wife, mother, teacher, and a survivor. My hope is that what I put down on paper will be a blessing to someone.

≫ TARIL GRAVELY ≪

God Gave Me Something Special

God Gave Me Something Special

It was a brutally cold, wind blowing, snow drifting time of year on the eve of my birth when my mother went into labor. My biological father brought the midwives to help my mother with the delivery. One of the midwives that came would later become my mother's sister-in-law. I arrived mid-morning on December 27, 1944. It was a hard birth and some people thought it was an odd birth because I was born with a veil on my face. It was a thin layer of skin from the hairline down to my nose. In those days, babies' eyes did not open up until the ninth day. When my eyes opened, the veil dropped, my mother wrapped it in a cloth and had someone to bury it. I always thought the veil meant voodoo or something bad, but I was wrong because God gave me the ability to see things before they actually happen in a vision, hear another conversation amongst people while having my own conversation and read people when looking through their eyes because your eyes are the mirror to your soul. If I see the bad in a person, I do not mistreat or hate them, but feed them with a long handle spoon.

My mother was so sick that the oldest midwife told her that she could not breastfeed me. However, one of the midwives

31

that recently gave birth nursed me until my mother was able to breastfeed me. My mother and I remained with her mother in Virginia until she married my stepfather. My mother left me with my grandmother until she died.

At the age of four years old, my mother came to get me to live with my stepfather and his children in North Carolina. While oftentimes crying, I felt sad and alone as if I were on the outside looking in because I missed my grandmother so much. It was an awkward situation that took me a while to get used to my mama, but I never got used to papa. I always knew my stepfather was not my father by the way he looked at me. I could see it in his eyes and could tell by his body language because we did not make a connection. Although I would ask my mother about my father, she would always tell me that I was living with him. I told her that he was not my real father. She would tell me, "If you don't shut your mouth and get out of here and find something to do, I am going to backslap you," so I found something to do inside or outside of the house. I remember being in grade school when first hearing a man's voice that would say, "I am your teacher." As a teenager, I began to have visions from God, which continued into womanhood. The voice that spoke to me was the voice of a man. I never told anyone about the visions or voice because they would not have understood. They would have thought I was actually talking to a man and no child should have to endure such humiliation. The need to find my father never left my mind, but I was responsible for my family. God began to teach me in my twenties.

My life started in a five-room shack. The shack did not have any lights or running water. When I met my new family, there were thirteen children that belonged to my stepfather and his first wife. My stepsisters helped me to fit in and feel wanted and sometimes free because of their embrace. They taught me about the farm by assigning chores such as the chicken house, pig pen, stable, and the pack house where they kept the tobacco. We were responsible for night work such as getting in firewood for the old cook stove, sweeping the hardwood floors and washday was on Wednesday. We had to wind the water from the well, heat it in a big black pot outside the bathhouse. We had ten tubs to bathe in and the girls would always go first, then the boys would take their baths later. We had fun just talking about the chores we had to do throughout the day. We had some really hard times when we went to bed hungry because there was only enough food to have three meals a day. If we got hungry between meals, we would eat fruit until our mother called us to eat supper. Although I was scared of the animals, my sisters and brothers let me know that was the way we lived to survive. As we grew up, we were able to bond through laughter and conversation. While we had misunderstandings and disagreements along the way, we were able to come back together and start talking to each other again. My brothers and sisters formed a spiritual bond because all of us believed and trusted in God. Although we had to walk to church, Mama and Papa were determined to get us there to hear preaching, praying, singing hymns and spirituals and shouting that would soothe the heart and fill the woods with an echo. I still sing those songs today, which brings back such precious memories. My mother always treated us the same in sickness and in health. Although I never heard the words "I Love You" from my mother or stepfather, I felt their love.

My mother gave me my birth certificate at the age of twenty in 1969. The birth certificate was created with my stepfather's name on it after my mother married my stepfather. Although it grieves my heart to know that my birth certificate was falsified, I still love my mother because she did it to protect me. As a child, I always knew my stepfather was not my father because when my biological father came to visit, I felt a closeness to him. At the age of nine, my biological father told me he loved me. I later found out my biological father was my stepfather's nephew.

While growing up, I was told Mama and Papa were sharecroppers. I learned the true meaning of the life of a sharecropper while working in the fields farming tobacco, which was considered the "bumper" crop, which required us to work from sunrise to sunset. We planted our own vegetables (corn, tomatoes, cucumbers, squash, potatoes, and turnip greens), we had two cows that produced our milk and butter, and three mules and one horse that pulled the plow to work the fields. My stepfather seemed to think the trees were planted by the slaves.

We canned fruits and vegetables such as pickled cucumbers and beets for the winter. We had fruit trees (apple, pear, and peach) and nut trees (black walnut and pecan). God supplied the earth with dewberries, blackberries, and wild strawberries, which we would pick on Sunday, the only day we had to rest. My mother would wash, cook, and can the fruit in half-gallon jars and quart jars to make cobblers, preserves, jellies, and jam for the winter. The fruit on the trees became our desserts for supper. We lived off the land that was raised by our hands.

Mama and Papa would take the tobacco to the warehouse to be sold by auctioneers while the heads of different tobacco companies such as RJ Reynolds would bid silently using various signs and gestures. The warehouse workers would weigh it, line it up on the warehouse floor for auctioneers to come and start the bid process. After the tobacco had been sold by the pound to different companies, and the overseer got his third, Mama and Papa would pay off outstanding debts such as clothes and shoes bought on credit.

In 1964 after my stepfather died, we worked the farm to pay off debts before going our separate ways to live our lives. My brothers and sisters went to work in factories, and some of them got married and moved out of state to work before retirement. There are five out of eighteen still living today. Although we suffer from different ailments because of our age, we still keep in touch. We have remained friends because of genuine love, which is the glue that has held us together. We come from a Godly family where we bonded from the heart. We were also raised to love each other and treat one another with kindness and respect as blood sisters and brothers. I still feel the bond in my heart up until the present time.

As time passed, I left the sharecropper's shack and married a man from Virginia. Remarkably, my youngest sister and I married two men from Virginia and lived in walking distance of one another. My husband was called into the ministry and became a minister, but her husband did not belong to the church.

The day I married my husband in Virginia, my mother gave me a hug and told me she wished me the best. I had never received a hug from the age of four years old to twenty years old until now. It is not what my mother said to me, it was the feeling I received from the hug, which was warm and soothing, causing me to become very emotional. The feeling was so intense, I began to cry uncontrollably while our families gathered around to comfort me and started asking questions such as What is wrong? Are you sick? Is you scared? It will be all right. Do you know about tonight? They thought I was scared because I was a virgin, but I already knew what I needed to know about getting married. God began to teach me in my twenties and has been my teacher throughout the years. I have also been blessed to have a long-term memory.

While I was growing up, I heard my mother say, "The only way you can wear white is to be a virgin because when you stand before God and the preacher, God wants you to be pure." I was extremely proud to stand before God and wear a white dress. After having my first child, I took my child to see my mother and she met me at the door. I put the baby in her arms and she cradled her and told my baby, "You were born from a virgin," with a gut laugh and said, "That is the way God would have it." She told me, "However many chaps you have, teach them that they were born to a virgin mother."

After having my daughter almost three years later, I had a miscarriage six days before going to visit my mother which was the last time I saw her alive. I told her that I did not want any more children because the loss was too painful. She spoke with a force when she told me, "You are going to have another child and he is going to be smart." Although I relied on it being another girl, about a month before having my son, God made it known to me that it was going to be a boy. My mind went back to what my mother told me when I had my son. As my son grew up, he was very smart. During my pregnancy, my body contracted several illnesses. In my second month, I got the mumps in May, the measles at the beginning of August, and the chicken pox in October. I was so sick and lost so much weight because I could not eat. Although I had no appetite, I continued to eat food through a straw, which became a liquid to drink so my child could receive the nutrients he needed. I would drink the broth of Chicken Noodle soup through a straw while my daughter would eat the noodles. I continued to take care of my daughter because she needed me, but I later found out that the mumps could have dropped meaning if the swelling had left out of my jaws and moved to my stomach causing infection it could have killed me and my child.

After going to the doctor, he told me to abort my baby because I would have to take care of the child for the rest of my life. The baby would be born brain dead, blind, and have to be fed and changed for the rest of his life. The baby would get older, but not grow. The doctor filled out the paperwork for me to have an abortion. After leaving the doctor's office on the way home, I shared with my husband what the doctor said about him wanting me to have an abortion. As soon as I got home, I ripped up the papers the doctor gave me about the abortion and put them in the trash. As I was ripping up the papers, I was asking God to stay with me, keep me and my baby. I asked God if it was His will to put everything the doctor said my child would be into smartness. I had a healthy baby boy born January 1, 1971, and his grandfather told me that he could see the sign on his forehead. When I went back to the doctor for my six-week checkup, I looked at the doctor and told him, "You wanted me to murder my baby. He can see, hear and eat and, in time, as he is growing, God is going to allow him to walk." The doctor said it was surprising to him because they found everything well with my son. My son grew up to be an intelligent and knowledgeable child.

At the age of four years old, he seemed to have a curiosity about the earth based on his questions and conversation. He was standing, looking up at the sky, and said, "I was just thinking that when you die, how you get to heaven?" He wanted to know which direction you take to get to heaven. He wanted to know if you go through the cloud or on the other side of the cloud to get to heaven. I told him, "We are on planet earth, and God created the earth in six days and on the seventh day He rested." He talked about how pretty the stars were in the sky. I told him that God hung the stars in the elements. I told him that we would go to sleep over here and wake up on the other side, resting in

God. He would always say, "It is pretty over there," and I would say,"It is beautiful, it is like no other place." He knew the devil was underneath the ground, but he did not know how the devil came into existence. I wanted him to know how heaven and hell came into existence. His curiosity got the best of me because he got so intense about it, it scared me. I told him, "I do not know, but ask your grandfather."

His grandfather was a very wise and informative man who was a God-fearing deacon in the church. His grandfather was able to answer the question for my son and began to develop a close bond with him because of the quality time they spent together over the years. While growing up, he became fascinated with taking things apart and putting them back together again. He grew up with an old soul because of his sense of awareness. It was as if he was born before his time. While he was growing up as a teenager and into a young man, I would tell him, "You don't know it until you know it for yourself." When he reached manhood, he told me "Now I know it all for myself," because God had come into his heart. God had put understanding in his heart and reasoning in his mind. He was a child of God, destined for greatness because he was blessed to make straight-A's throughout elementary, middle and high school. He was accepted to several colleges, but he chose to attend DeVry Institute of Technology in Decatur, Georgia, to fulfill his dream of becoming a Computer Engineer. He made the Dean's list the entire time he worked toward his bachelor's and master's degrees. He is married with three children and a grandchild. Although my daughter was smart growing up in every way, her desire was to graduate from high school and get a job. She is married with a daughter. She and her daughter are working and doing very well. We love and support our children, grandchildren and great-grandchild. We are very proud of their accomplishments.

While I did not get to retire because the doctor took me out of work due to several illnesses during my pregnancy, I always wanted to be a baby's nurse, known as a pediatrician. God granted me that wish by allowing me to keep children in the community for their parents while they worked. I was a babysitter for over thirty children and truly enjoyed every moment of taking care of them and teaching them fundamental and foundational skills to thrive and survive in life. I will always cherish the precious memories spent watching them grow up, helping them solve problems, and simply having a conversation. They are considered my extended family and often times come back to visit and share how they appreciate me for teaching them life's lessons that they are passing on to their children, which is a blessing through and by God.

Although I live in Virginia, my memories often bring me back to the farm in North Carolina. I really love farm living because on a Sunday afternoon we would sit on the porch, breathing in fresh air, listening to chickens cackle and the purity of running water in a creek while watching the cows, mules, and horses graze in the open space representing freedom.

Taril Gravely is a native of Martinsville, VA. She is a graduate of North Carolina Agricultural and Technical State University. She is a humanitarian, activist, educator, and poet who enjoys writing, event planning, traveling and spending time with family. Her talents as a mentor, facilitator, care giver, avid reader, and music connoisseur aspire her to be an author, motivational speaker and documentarian. Taril is the creator of TMG Enterprises whose founding principle is based on "the desire to inspire people to create passion with purpose."

Quiet Strength

She is an amazing God-fearing, kind-spirited
woman that comes from humble beginnings
with no endings

She is a storyteller by nature and a caregiver
through and by God

She has a vivid imagination that enables her to
paint pictures in her mind all the time

She has endured pain and sorrow that left her
hollow and is a powerful prayer warrior

Her beautiful smile lights up a room like a
Christmas tree priceless

The words of wisdom glow on her face and flows
from her tongue with such mercy and grace

She praises God Almighty down on her knees
while clapping glad hands with a plea that
everything will be all right with all her might

Her calling as a servant of God was that she
loved children near and far

Taril Gravely

You could not leave her house without
something to eat even if it's a small sweet treat

She is the glue that holds the family together

She has obtained the highest diploma in the
land by searching God's holy command, which
has given her the insight to continuously fight

Her life will live on within the hearts of so
many until the end

*"In all things I have shown you that by working
hard in this way we must help the weak and
remember the words of the Lord Jesus, how he
himself said, 'It is more blessed to give than to
receive,"* — Acts 20:35

Love Always,
Taril Gravely

≫ KIMBERLLI HOLLINGS ≪

Thank You

Thank You

Today is graduation day and the house is a little hectic. Everyone is running around, trying to get ready. See, today is very special because not only am I graduating with my master's degree, but my oldest stepson is graduating from high school. Our family has to split up in order to be able to attend both ceremonies. So, my husband and stepdaughter are going to my stepson's graduation, and my daughter, son, and husband's cousin—who has become one of my closest friends—are coming to my graduation.

I grab my cap and gown and keys, and we run out the door and jump in the car. As I am driving to the school's campus, I am feeling a level of accomplishment and thankfulness because for so many reasons, I was not supposed to achieve this goal. My life was not set up for much success. Many would say I have defied the odds. I've had a very difficult life, from being homeless, molested, and raped to feeling unloved and unwanted by my parents.

When we arrive at the school, most of the other graduates were already there. We start putting on our caps and gowns, and helping each other to get ready. We gather around the spiral staircase leading up to the auditorium where the ceremony is to take place. We pose for pictures. We started out with twelve classmates, but by graduation there are only ten of us receiving our master's degrees today. I'm elated I have made it this far when the odds of my life were stacked against me.

As I sit on the stage, listening to the speakers, I look out into the sea of friends and families assembled for us. They are smiling and some are crying because they are so proud of us. I look at my daughter and son and I know that they are proud of their mother.

I begin to think about some of the most difficult times in my life. I remember when my son was only four months old when my mother and stepdad kicked me out of the house. They were having an argument that escalated to my stepdad beating my mother. When I jumped in to try to pull him off her, she told me to stay out of it and then told me to get out of their house and to never come back. I had nowhere to go. My son and I were now homeless. In that moment, I felt like my mother did not care about me or her grandson. I stayed in a hotel room and then ended up staying with a friend and her dad, where we slept in their basement on a couch. This was the lowest I'd ever felt in my life. That was the moment I became determined I was going to provide a life of stability and love for my child because this was something I had never had.

The speaker calls my name. I walk across the stage and shake her hand as she hands me my degree. I turn slightly to the right to face the photographer to have my picture taken before returning to my seat. As I watch others receive their degrees, tears are forming in my eyes; I am proud of myself. This journey was only made possible because of my family, which now consists of my husband and our children. I am married to a wonderful man and his family is so supportive of us. He made sure I had everything I needed to be successful in school and he is the reason I graduated. He watched the kids so I could study and attend classes. And when he had to work, his mother stepped in and she watched our children for us. He is a true blessing to me and our children.

Now the last person is walking up to get their degree and I am remembering meeting my husband. After all the things I had been through in my life, I was sure love wasn't in the plan for my life. I have had many failed relationships. Well, most of them weren't relationships, they were just men who wanted to be with me, but not stay with me. In the beginning, when my husband showed his love for me, it was difficult for me to trust his love. I was scared and it didn't feel normal to me. Pain and hurt were my normal. Feeling alone and being alone were normal to me. Now I'm constantly surrounded by love and people who choose to be with me. It was weird. It was uncomfortable at times. It really took me some time to adjust to this new normal.

After the ceremony we return to the house. My husband has planned this big graduation cookout for my stepson and me. We have a quaint three-bedroom, one-and-one-half-bath brick home with cute peach-colored shutters around the windows. Our home sits in a cul-de-sac with only three other homes on the street. We have a very steep driveway because our home sits low, almost as if it's in a ditch. We use the back door entrance most of the time to come in and out of our house. Off from the back door are a small patio, a huge back yard with lots of woods behind it, the kids' trampoline, a lawn table and chairs, and a grill.

I go in the house to change clothes and start prepping the food. We are having ribs, chicken, pork chops, hamburgers and hot dogs with all the trimmings, baked beans, salad, deviled eggs, and potato salad. We have a lot of guests coming to the house today.

Off from my kitchen is the dining room and den combo. It's a long room and on one side of the room stands a dining room table with four chairs and opposite the dining room is the den area. I have a light green sofa and love seat with a coffee table. The flat screen TV sits in front of the sofa and coffee table. I have a stereo system that sits next to the TV stand. I walk over to the stereo and pop in a Mary J. Blige CD. I have loved Mary J. Blige because her music spoke to me during some of the lowest points in my life. Now when I listen to her, I no longer cry, but her music helps to keep me humble because it reminds me of how I felt during that time. So now I'm singing and dancing around. I am dicing onions and bell peppers to put in my baked beans. My husband and stepchildren have just arrived at the house and we are all talking and laughing. Now some guests are starting to arrive so my husband moves the stereo system outside and he changes the music to some old school '80s jams. We are doing some of the old dances from back then. I look around at all of our guests and my family, and I smile. I'm happy. This is definitely one of the happiest moments of my life. Children are running around and jumping on the trampoline. Grownups are laughing and enjoying alcoholic beverages and the music is loud and bumping.

Twenty years ago when my son and I were homeless, I couldn't have imagined we would be here at this moment. I have been through so much in my life. My journey was hard and difficult. I had to keep pushing because once I had my son it was no longer about my life, but the kind of life I wanted to provide for him. There were many people who helped me in my life. My friends and their families were always there for me. Times when life was difficult at home, it was my friends that gave me a safe haven. They were very instrumental for my success in life. They were family.

It's getting late and the guests are beginning to leave. I help my husband and children bring in all the food from outside and we put everything up. My husband is still outside talking to his cousins and I go to our bedroom to get ready for bed. I walk over to my bed and kneel down on my knees. With tears flowing from eyes, I bow my head, clasp my hands, and say, "Thank you."

My name is Kimberlli Hollings. I was born in Cleveland, Ohio, but raised in Georgia. I am a wife, mother of five, and grandmother. I have a blended family and some people have compared us to the Huxtables from *The Cosby Show*. My family and I live in Georgia. We are a very close family and our children are some of the most creative and funniest people you'd ever want to meet.

I obtained a Bachelor's Degree in Business from Fort Valley State University and a Master's Degree from Wesleyan College. In my spare time, I like to write, read, and watch romantic movies. On my blog, "Evolving Lives – Lives Evolving," I try to use the lessons I have learned and my experiences to help others start their journey of healing and living their purpose.

9520

"To Tell The Truth"

⚜ CAROLYN HOUSE ⚜

9520
"To Tell The Truth"

From 1956 to 1968, there was a television program called *To Tell The Truth*, a classic game show in which a person of some notoriety and two impostors try to match wits with a panel of four celebrities. The object of the game is to try to fool the celebrities into voting for the two impostors. After a series of questions asked by the four celebrities, the contestant would guess which one was telling the truth. Sometimes, the special guest was able to act and answer questions skillfully enough to fool the contestants. For many years, I fooled the contestants. Now, at the very ripe age of fifty-two, I yearn to tell the truth. It is said, "Confession is good for the soul," of which I'm a firm believer.

Picture a community of Afro-Americans who worked hard to keep a middle-class lifestyle. Residents took pride in their houses and neighborhood. Behind the doors, however, secrets and hidden fetishes resided in this upstanding community. During the late seventies, cocaine became the drug of choice for those who could afford it. Negroes called it the white man's high. Shortly afterward, a cheaper version called crack was produced. It spread rapidly like

53

cancer, gossip, or a cheap bottle of wine among alcoholics. The neighborhood, which was surrounded with pride and convictions, had now reversed into a living hell. Many houses opened their doors to drug addicts and drug dealers. Families were being torn apart; children were neglected during the era of crack cocaine. Adult females, who once had dignity and self-respect, were now using their bodies for drugs. It became common for men to pay for a cheap companion who provided sexual favors while smoking crack.

Annette's story began when she was a young girl, living in an upscale residential area where everyone knew one another. She did not look like most kids. Her dark, deep brown skin color caused many to joke and speak negative words to discredit her ability to achieve self-esteem, trust, and emotional stability. Those close to her made the most accusations: "You so black, fat with no shape, no booty, and nappy hair." She laughed at their derogatory antics, never displaying any emotion of hurt. As time passed on, the words became etched in her bosom; she found herself searching for an identity. That identity was found with the guys in the neighborhood. She did not have to worry about being cute and feminine, she was accepted for who she was. The new friends were known criminals who taught her everything they knew. She even became their alibi when a crime was committed. One of the guys began to sell drugs, putting everyone on board as a drug dealer, except for her.

As time went on, Annette lost the weight and was looking fly. The guys felt like she abandoned their friendship to become a beautiful young lady who attracted a different class of fellows. One man, in particular, caught her attention. He soon became the father of her son. By this time, she was experimenting with cocaine and other narcotic drugs. It did not take long before her life began to spiral out of control. She found herself staying at the crack house for days, leaving her son in the care of her mom and grandmother. Years of addiction landed her in quandaries such as jail, selling drugs, and living at 9520 for years. Unfortunately, her reputation followed outside the community as a woman who smoked crack, with the ability to sell more drugs than the sober dealers. She was respected by many, even top gang officials. Her protection proceeded farther than she ever imagined. There were several organizations that tried to hire her to help build their drug cartels. One board member of a well-known street gang kept her as his personal assistant, which meant she was untouchable.

Annette dated a guy that was addicted to cocaine who provided her with the substance for many years prior to her selling drugs. He also dabbled in selling drugs, too, however his habit caused him to use the product that was supposedly being sold; the end result was not pretty. The very first day of employment, he was paid in advance. His mom was also given money, food, and alcohol. Later that day, Annette got word that her boyfriend was hiding from this wicked man that exuded street power and forces. His name was very well-known in the community with immense fear that followed.

The next day, Annette was in the restaurant when she heard someone say "LA." She turned around and said, "So you're LA everyone is afraid of."

"You should be scared, too," he replied.

"I don't fear any man, only God."

He looked to his crew. "Who is this woman and where did she come from?" When LA's friend shouted, "That's Craig's lady," he looked very surprised.

He turned his attention back to Annette. "I'm sorry, but I'm going to have to make a move on your guy."

"Why? You knew Craig had a habit, but you took a chance anyway; that's on you."

"Nobody talks to me like that, but for some reason, I like you," he said and proceeded to pay for her food.

Annette told him, "Let me help. I can make money back, plus pay you extra."

He smirked. "That's impossible!" He paused and said, "I'll be in touch."

The next day, LA arranged a meeting with Annette outside on a busy public street with security posted on every corner, just in case something went wrong.

"I did a resume on you," said the dashing drug dealer, "and not one person had anything bad to say about you. If I give you a chance, you will be responsible for the whole package." He went on to say, "Whatever you say your due date is I expect my money on that day. Your word is your bond. If you say next month, on the fifteenth, I expect to get paid on that day."

Annette didn't budge. "I'll have your money by tonight," she told him and she did.

From that moment on, 9520 was on the map. Annette sold thousands of dollars of drugs continuously for years and LA, who supplied her stashed, became her secret lover.

Annette's identity was soon discovered in the streets, which provoked jealousy and envy. Now the police got word of her involvement with the drug organization, but they knew she was just a peddler working for a larger fish. No one was to be trusted, not even her own boyfriend. He stole rocks whenever he could, along with his brother and girlfriend. It became a game. Once she got wind of the thievery, she would leave moth balls wrapped like rocks. Everyone in the entire household had some type of addiction, whether it was alcohol, heroin or crack. Seven adults and three children lived in a three-bedroom home in the middle of a beautiful community. The house was known for many miles as a place to smoke, drink, and purchase narcotics. The house was discussed at every CAPS meeting. The neighbors thought she was there taking care of the elderly lady who owned the house. She always was polite, never walked the streets, and only came out late at night, so the neighbors would not see her movements. During the day, she used other people to distribute the rocks. She was wise; she always presented a different persona in public.

The house became out of control. All sorts of people were coming in and out, looking to buy drugs and a place to get high. Fights erupted all the time, leaving splattered blood on the carpet and walls. Craig's brother died in the house one night after he had gone out snorting dope. Months later, the alcohol began to have its effect on his mother. She would pass out on the floor unconscious until Annette helped her to bed. However, Ms. J continued to drink and eat less. Actually, there was never any food in the house. The home smelled like dirt, and stale cigarette smoke, the carpet was filthy with all sorts of spills and bodily fluids. The bathroom was small and dirty with urine on the floor and toilet seat. Cigarette butts and ashes littered the floor. The shower was only used by Annette and she cleaned the bathroom before each use. After she showered, the fresh smell of body wash and perfume lingered for a little while until the lingering odor from the house overpowered the sweet aroma. She would not leave the premises to go home to a clean four-bedroom home where she was safe and had food.

Living at 9520, Annette lost several pants sizes, which troubled her mom. On a regular, her mother picked her up to feed her and take her to the show. By the grace of God, the contents of her purse were never revealed. She left the house with hundreds of dollars and enough drugs to get the entire theater high. On one particular occasion, she had $5,000-worth of rocks in her purse while going out to eat and shop with her mom, who happened to be a minister.

The prayers of her family and church members began to bring a change in Annette's life. One day, her mom called to tell her about a dream God had given her.

"The police are coming and everything will be put on you. Get out that *house!*" her mom said.

Annette waited a week, and during the course of that time, things were out of control. She became fearful for her life. The word on the street was that a hit was placed on her. That night, she gave her life back to Christ. She made sure the kids at 9520 had food to eat and attempted to turn in all the drugs. She ignored the witness in her spirit to call a cab and go home.

Annette fell asleep early that morning, and a few hours later, the police were at the door. There was no special lock on the door, but they could not break down the door. It took several attempts to wake her before she finally got up. The police finally made their entry and served her with a warrant. Their search did not turn up anything until one officer went outside. When he returned, he went straight to the stash hidden in the attic. There he found one hundred grams of packaged rocks ready for distribution and a sawed-off shotgun. Immediately, the handcuffs were placed on her wrists with a detective walking her to the car. Neighbors peered through their curtains, witnessing her walk of embarrassment and shame. The charge given was twenty-five grams of cocaine with the intent to distribute and a sawed-off shotgun. The time faced was fifteen to thirty years with no probation. This was a class X felony, a serious offense, that carried mandatory sentencing. The bond was set at $10,000 cash, with no percentage; the full amount. Her grandmother was able to bond her out with no problem. It took several days for the release and the paperwork to be processed before she could return home with a long year of court appearances.

⤳

Prior to my last court date, my grandmother passed. She died in my arms on 95th Street in transit to the hospital. Erma Gray gave me my freedom before she left this earth. I sat there confused as to why she had to leave before seeing my transformation. Today, I'm an ordained minister, with two degrees, of which one proudly obtained from Roosevelt University. My mission is to help those achieve the unachievable, such as myself. Life decisions can lead you down a path of destruction, however, with the help of God, you can make it!

Carolyn House is a lover of God's people, young and old. She sets the course of a servant to assist those in need. She works diligently in the communities with the goals of becoming an Alderman in her ward. As an ordained minister, she travels around the United States, ministering to those willing to hear the voice of God. The wrong decisions of the past cultivated who she has become today—a woman with two degrees, an ordained minister by the renowned Apostle John Eckhardt and a community activist. She has no regrets and no shame, just grateful she made it through.

≫ JILL HOWARD ≪

When the Odds Are Against You—Rebel!

When the Odds are Against You—Rebel!

I was a rebel growing up. According to statistics, I was not supposed to make it. In my immediate family, I was considered the "black sheep" because my behavior did not fit that of the family in which I was raised. My parents were successful. Momma was a successful head secretary for one of the most prestigious high schools in the country, and Daddy was a brilliant businessman who owned a thriving construction company. Momma always drove nice luxury cars and I cannot remember a time when money was an issue.

However, there was trouble in my parents' marriage that seemed to be brushed under the rug. Their late night arguments that my sisters seemed to sleep right through kept me up late at night. I absolutely adored Daddy, but I could never understand why he would hit on Momma. One night, Momma decided enough was enough and made a plan to end the marriage. My daddy, who meant the world to me, was no longer in my world. I could not understand why I could not see my father. I later found out that restraining orders were issued, which were probably best for the safety of my mother, but at thirteen years old, I could not understand.

I tested and was accepted into the prestigious school where Momma worked and I was expected to perform. Instead, I did no work, got into fights, and completely embarrassed my mother. This was the beginning of the embarrassment I would cause my mother.

By age fourteen, I met a boy who treated me the exact way Daddy treated Momma. He made sure he treated me nicely and gave me gifts, but then he would get upset and want to fight me. I didn't understand why, I thought it was love, especially considering that the only other man I adored had done the exact thing to the woman he loved (Momma). This boy told me he loved me and he was the only male in my life since Daddy was gone.

Before my fifteenth birthday, I was pregnant. PREGNANT! What did this mean exactly? I had sex one time and it was absolutely painful and unenjoyable. How could I be pregnant? Within the first trimester, I lost the baby. Around my sixteenth birthday, I found I was pregnant again. Sixteen and pregnant. This time I knew what it meant to be pregnant and it was normal for my boyfriend and me to fight and then have sex. Not only was I involved in teen dating domestic violence, I was now a teen mother. I knew I needed to stay healthy so I would not lose my baby so I broke up with my boyfriend and did what I thought would bring me the less stress...I dropped out of school.

Momma was very displeased with my decisions. But with Daddy being gone, I knew I needed to be able to provide for my son. I worked a full-time job and moved into my own apartment. I didn't have a car and had to walk about three miles to work. I had to pay for a babysitter and could barely afford my bills. Eventually, I lost my apartment, and my son and I were homeless. Going back to Momma's house was not an option. I had to figure life out. My son and I lived from house to house until my eighteenth birthday when I could get an apartment legally since I was of age. My son was my inspiration. He was my reason for living. Every decision I made from the time he entered into the world was to give him the best life. I worked tirelessly to pay my bills and purchase a car. Once I got a car, I went back to school, got my GED, and began college.

Life was finally on the upswing. I started my own relationship with my father, I had a good job, my own apartment, a car, my son was happy and healthy, and I was attending college. One day I received a call from my son's father who wanted to spend time with him. I did not trust his father taking him, so I told him he could come to my new home and hang out with my son. This was a huge mistake. I could not get him to leave. He began taking my car, causing me to miss work, and reverted to abusing me. All the hard work it took me to get to the place where I was in my life seemed to be shattered. I began smoking marijuana to help me cope with the stress and pain, but this also caused me to lose my job. I got hurt at work and my employer sent me to get checked. A part of that check was a drug test in which I failed. Although I had not smoked that day, the marijuana was in my system.

Things began to quickly spiral downhill. My son's father was providing for us with drug money and with that lifestyle came many negative outcomes. He was in and out of jail and my car was seized by the police because he took the police on a high-speed chase in it. Eventually, I dropped out of college and by my twentieth birthday, I was pregnant with my second son. The verbal and physical abuse escalated and, at one point, death flashed before my eyes. I was badly beaten and the same man (my father), who physically abused my mother, had come to visit me and had to lift me out of the bedroom wall that I had been thrown through.

Once my second son was born, I moved to an apartment that was closer to my mother with the hopes of us developing a new relationship. She was actually glad to have my sons around and quickly fell in love with the newest addition to the family. I was now a responsible, respectable young woman and had a new perspective on life. Although the decisions I made in life made things difficult for me each day, I worked really hard to change my sons' and my outcome in life.

By the time I was twenty-one years old, I made the decision to move to the capital city of my state. I packed up a U-Haul and my sons and moved to a city where I knew no one. I had not found a job prior to going, but I had enough money to pay two months' rent on my apartment, which gave me sixty days to find a job and have money to pay my bills.

Today, I am a successful entrepreneur, a mother of six amazing children, three which I birthed and three that are my husband's children I raised as my own. I have experienced multiple levels of success in corporate America. My oldest son, whom I birthed at sixteen years old, will be graduating from one of the top schools in our area and has a scholarship to attend college where he will continue his career in football. All of my children are great kids and I am blessed to mother each of them.

I am a firm believer in what you believe is what you can achieve. No matter what your story may be, you can overcome all things. Faith, hard work, dedication, and a willingness to change is how I've successfully made a better life for my children and me. I refused to be a statistic or allow my children to be statistics. There are a few things I'm going to share to help you with this along the way!

When the Odds are Against You—Rebel!

1. Faith.

There is a saying that "There is light at the end of the tunnel." I believe that as long as there is faith the size of a mustard seed and a little hope, then there will be a bright side to all stories. But you have to believe it for yourself.

2. Believe in yourself, even when others don't.

You do this by first making the decision that you want something different, no matter what your situation is. Maybe you want better grades, or to develop a better relationship with a family member. Maybe you would like to return to school or play a sport, or an instrument, or rap, or maybe you're an aspiring actress or an entrepreneur or the next President of the United States. Maybe you would like to be a teacher, nurse, police officer, doctor, biochemist, scientist or work on finding a cure for cancer. Whatever you would like to do is possible if you put your mind to it!

3. Hard Work!

For the majority of people, you have to work to get what you need and want in life. If you want to be above the average then you have to really work hard. This means you may not be able to do things that others do. You may have to turn down hanging out with friends, or other things that may take up too much of your time like social media use and watching television. Always think that there is someone else that may be better at something than you, so to stay in the race you may have to work a little bit harder than everyone else.

4. Be Dedicated.

No one can meet your heart's desires. You have to want it for yourself. Once you decide what you want, you have to be dedicated and committed to doing the things that are necessary to meet your goals, dream and heart's desires.

5. Give Back!

Trust me, I had no idea I would be where I am today when I was sleeping from couch to couch with my son. Now I give back to homeless teen moms and young mothers who just need a little extra push through the non-profit organization Mothers Helping Mothers, Inc. (MHM) out of Columbus, Ohio. MHM provides housing, childcare, job placement, food pantry, diapers, wipes and clothing to women who are walking in the shoes that I once walked in. Giving back is vital for the future of our communities.

Find an area in your community where you can give back and do it! It may be cutting a sick or elderly person's grass, walking a dog for someone who is unable, serving at a food pantry, going to a nursing home and playing a game or helping someone who is being bullied.

Whatever you decide to do, giving back makes your heart lighter and is good service to those who you are helping.

6. Give thanks!

Give thanks always, all year-round. Even in your darkest moments, if you woke up you have something to be thankful for. If you have food to eat, then you have something to be thankful for. No matter how good or bad life may be, give thanks and always keep in mind that there is light at the end of the tunnel.

7. *Forgive.*

LET IT GO! Whoever hurt you, caused you any pain or anger; do not hold grudges, do not carry that pain, but LET IT GO! Forgive those who talk about you, lie on you, misuse you, and use you. Forgiveness does not mean you allow people to continuously hurt you, it just means that you make the decision to not carry it in your heart so you can be free. The moment you decide not to forgive is the moment you decide you don't want more in your life. You can only go so far in life carrying unfairness and a heavy heart. Once you let it go, the sky's the limit.

Jill has accomplished multiple levels of success in corporate America including technical writing, policies and procedures development for the finance/accounting office of a major Ohio Medicare payer. She understands that the development of a plan or business requires a process and has the skill required to develop, forecast and implement a plan of action that produces results.

Jill was also on the ground floor of the MyCare Ohio integration which is historical in the healthcare industry. The MyCare integration took the Medicare insurance plan with all of its rules, regulations, laws, payment scales and merged it with Ohio Medicaid's rules, regulations, laws, payment scales which was both exciting and complicated. Jill was on the Ohio team that worked with all the other participating MyCare Ohio insurance payers, to devise a plan that would streamline the processing and payment of claims.

Jill's passion for the elderly came from taking care of her grandfather as a young girl which led her to becoming a care provider for the elderly by the age of eighteen. She was a State Tested Nursing Assistant for a four-year duration but quickly learned that she needed to be in a position of change. Jill's skills in her administrative and executive roles paired with her experience and passion to care for the Elderly is what JATD Senior Care and Consulting was birthed from. "I've always been passionate for the elderly" stated thirty-three-year-old Jill Howard. "Our elders are who paved the way for many generation including my own. They are someone's mother, father, aunt or uncle. All elders regardless of income bracket, race, nationality, background or creed deserve quality care and JATD is here for that reason and that reason alone."

"We stand strong on our core values, patience, kindness, humility, selflessness, integrity, gentleness."
– Jill Howard

≫ CATHEY W. LAW ≪

The Miracle is in What's Left

The Miracle is in What's Left

1965 was a very important time in the history of Civil Rights and the little town of Coden, Alabama had to be just as racially divided as the rest of the South. I could imagine with all of that racial unrest, my expectant parents were on a roller coaster ride of emotions. With the assassination of Malcolm X in February to the iconic Selma March later that spring, I could only imagine the tension in the air. I could imagine they were excited about the possibility of being able to add a son to the household currently filled with six girls. This would actually be the ninth birth for my parents, but my sister, Zenobia, and brother, Leo, Jr., also known as Bubba, died as infants. I could imagine that as the seasons moved from spring to summer and finally winter, my sisters were equally excited and preparing to welcome another sibling.

For my oldest sister, there would be an eighteen-year gap between her and her new sister or brother. She was preparing to be the first of the sisters to go to college. The other sisters ranged from toddlers to high school, so I could imagine the house was filled with school activities, church events, parties, and family gatherings. On Christmas Eve, I could imagine the tree was decorated since Mom was nine months pregnant and Dad, my aunts, and grandmother took over the kitchen that year. On Christmas Day, I could imagine they attended church service at our local church, Coleman Chapel A.M.E Zion . Later that day I imagine the entire family gathering to celebrate Christmas 1965 with lots of food, laughter and love. As they day wound to a close, I imagine no one knew this would be their last time celebrating in this manner. I could imagine Mom retiring early because she was exhausted from the day's excitement.

Sunday, December 26, 1965, I could imagine my mother›s water broke early that morning and she kissed each of my sisters before leaving for the hospital with Dad. I could imagine Dad returned home much later that day and was greeted by six eager faces to hear the announcement of whether they had a new baby brother or sister. It wasn't the news anyone could have imagined. Dad said, "You no longer have a mother, but you have a beautiful baby sister." My mother died giving me life or as my now tattered birth certificate reads: *This infant's mother expired on December 26, 1965. Ironically, my birth certificate did not reveal much else. Of course it had my mother and fathers names, occupation, age, etc. However, no mention of my time of birth or weight.*

Now five years old, I lived with Aunt Louise and her husband down the street from Dad and my siblings. I knew in my spirit it was odd that I didn't live with my siblings, but I never wanted to ask too many details around my mother's death. I told myself that if I asked it would cause too much pain for Dad and my sisters, so I tried to be really quiet, almost invisible and never asked too many questions. It was around this age that I first heard the full story after Dad came home from the hospital. In the midst of grieving and planning a funeral, Dad had to quickly figure out how he was going to raise six girls and a newborn.

There was an emergency family meeting with my aunts and uncles from both Mom's and Dad's sides of the family. Decisions had to be made, such as naming the baby and deciding which village would step in and help raise not only me, but my two youngest siblings who were three and four years old at the time. The meeting convened and it was decided I would take a version of my mother's first name and a version of my grandmother's first name as a middle name. This was where it got interesting. My oldest sister, who could not attend the family meeting, had secretly petitioned Dad for a name and that is how I ended up with two middle names. It was also decided at this meeting that Aunt Louise on Dad's side would raise me, but per the storyteller, my oldest sister and everyone wanted "the baby."

Luckily, Aunt Louise, affectionately known as Ise, lived two minutes down the street from Dad, so I was never far from my family. Actually, my oldest sister begged to stay home from college to raise me, but thankfully Dad wasn't having it. My siblings closest to me in age went to live with my aunt in Mobile, Alabama, which was thirty minutes from Coden, but we saw one another every weekend. Even as a young child, I was keenly aware of the whispers and stares from family members and complete strangers in the community. Everyone around me wanted to take a peek at Catherine's baby. How was she doing? Who did she look like? How would she turn out?

As a child myself, I had no idea of the depth of the pain and heartache my family experienced after my mother died. Each of my sisters experienced her death through different lenses based on their age and, although they lived with our dad, they surely were hurting terribly. There is nothing like a mother's love, but Dad dedicated his life to all his girls and he did an amazing job.

In my formative years, my void was filled somewhat through Aunt Ise, who made sure I knew I was loved. In hindsight, we were poor as dirt, but I never noticed that because her love made me feel rich. I was a happy-go-lucky kid who enjoyed riding my bike, playing jump rope and jacks. I was a voracious reader and by the time I entered Head Start at four years old, I was reading on a third-grade level. I loved picking blackberries off the vine and climbing my grandmother's fig tree to eat figs until my stomach ached. I was enjoying being a kid and, despite my circumstances, I was happy. However, all that was about to change.

Shortly around the age of five or six, Aunt Ise began to work with foster families and a steady stream of kids started living with us. Sometimes there would be one child or other times an entire family often staying for a few weeks to several months. It was great for me because, in addition to having my big sisters, I now had this large extended family to play with. The Smith's came to stay with us in 1971. There were three girls who were close in age to me and two boys were probably in their early teens. This was the largest family yet to move in with us and our house was tiny. A small, white-framed house with a front porch, three bedrooms, a family room, and a kitchen, with one bathroom off the back porch. The girls and I shared one bedroom and the boys slept in the room with my uncle.

It started off fine and we all got along well. We went to school together, played, and attended church together on Sundays. I could be described as being *raised in the church* so Sundays we were in the house of the Lord all day. My day started early with Sunday school, 11:00 am service and sometimes evening service, either at my home church, my mother's family church or another local community church. For such a small community, there was never a shortage of places to worship. Aunt Ise was very active in the church so sometimes she had to attend various meetings. Once the Smith's arrived, I was allowed to stay at home and not attend the many missionary board or deaconess meetings with her.

I don't recall how it happened, but one day I was asked to play a new game. This new game was played on the back porch and it involved the oldest boy. I was encouraged by the other brother and even some of the sisters. Nothing about it felt right, but because the others watched and encouraged him, I thought maybe it was indeed a game. One of the sisters asked if she could participate and I recall the brother telling her, "No, Mama said not to do it with your sisters." I don't know how long this went on, but it seemed like every time Aunt Ise was out of the house, I was summoned to play our secret game. I don't know why I felt obligated to keep this secret from my aunt and uncle, but I did for a while. However, one day, something I said in the presence of Aunt Ise broke the evil cycle. I immediately knew something was wrong. The expression on her face told me so.

After that, things moved very swiftly. Dad was immediately called and I went to stay with him and my sisters a few days. When I returned, the entire Smith family had moved and several years later, I later learned that Social Services had been called.

It is said that time heals all wounds and to some extent it does. The wound has healed, but the scar remains. Things eventually moved back to "normal," but I never felt like a child again and a poor black child in 1972 certainly was not able to have any counseling. I became more of an introvert and chose to escape the pain by reading more and talking to my dolls and imaginary friends. The miracle in what was left is that I am here today. I know that it was the grace of God and the many family members who covered me in prayer, kept me encouraged, hopeful and strong-willed enough to feel I could overcome any obstacle. I would need that covering in the years to come.

Cathey W. Law

Cathey W. Law is Certified Life Coach, Keynote Speaker and Human Resources Executive. The president of Renewed Vision Empowerment Institute, a life and executive coaching firm, she specializes in helping women discover the course to take them to their destiny. She holds a BS in Industrial Psychology and a Masters in Human Resources Management. Visit her company website at www.renewedvisionempowermentinstitute.com.

≫ L'TARRA MOORE ≪

It Will Be Done!

It Will Be Done!

Several years ago a certain scripture kept coming to my attention—in Bible study, in worship service, in my morning devotional readings—the same scripture over and over. One day I decided to really read it. The scripture was Isaiah 55: 9-11, *"As the heavens are higher than the earth, so are my ways higher than your ways and my thoughts than your thoughts. As the rain and the snow come down from heaven, and do not return to it without watering the earth and making it bud and flourish, so that it yields seed for the sower and bread for the eater, so is my word that goes out from my mouth: It will not return to me empty, but will accomplish what I desire and achieve the purpose for which I sent it."* After reading it, I said to myself, "Okay. Got it," and went on about my business.

The next day, there it was again, while I was listening to a sermon. I exclaimed, "What am I supposed to get from this scripture?" I sat down with paper, pen, Bible, and commentary like I was taught in Bible study and read over the scripture and the commentary on it.

This was what I understood from my study of this passage: God's ways and thoughts are higher than ours. Because I am a visual person, I started thinking about being at the airport and watching planes ascending into the sky, so high until it is out of sight. And I thought about being in the plane and how we ascend into the sky. The higher we get everything gets smaller until you can't see it anymore. And the thing is, as high as we go into the sky, we are nowhere near Heaven. God's thoughts and ways are as high as the Heavens. Wow! When you really think about it, that is a great illustration! Now here comes the part that really blows me away! A metaphor. This passage of scripture uses illustration so I can visualize what is being said, bringing it home with a metaphor (a figure of speech that refers to something as being the same as another thing for rhetorical (repetition) effect. It may provide clarity or identify hidden similarities between two ideas). God's promise to us leaves God's mouth with a purpose. His promise will not return to Him until it fulfills its purpose. I finally realized what God wanted me to know and understand from this scripture. He wanted me to know that what He promised us, it will happen, IT WILL BE DONE.

A couple of years later, I realized God was preparing me for a major event in my life: my father having a major stroke. The day of my father's stroke, he came into my office and asked me to type something for him.

I asked him, "When do you need this?"

He looked back and said, "Yesterday," and walked off.

I was on my way to lunch and said, "I'll do it when I get back." But with God's grace, I quickly decided to take care of what he asked.

After I finished, I went over to my father's office and did not see him sitting at his desk. As I started out the door, I heard a rustling sound on the floor. I turned around, stepped to the side only to see my father lying on the floor trying to get up. I ran to the door of his office, screamed for help and ran back to him. The Chief of Staff ran in behind me and called 911. The next thing I knew, the security officer was there also. We were talking to Dad to let him know that we were there.

When we got to the hospital, everything was happening so fast. One person was saying, "Mr. Moore, how are you feeling?"

While another was asking, "Can you tell me what happened?"

"What medications is he taking?"

"Does he have this and that?"

It was all so much! One of the things I remember so clearly was that the doctors needed to know how long it was after he left my office and I found him. The doctors explained that with stroke patients, there is a three-hour window of time (The Golden Window) where they can give medicine to dissolve the clot that caused the stroke. After that window of time, you cannot receive the medicine. All I kept thinking was, *Jesus! My dad had a stroke! Lord, have mercy!* I am thankful to have found my father when I did. Several months later, my father was back on his feet and slowly healing.

That was a tough time in my life. To see my father lying on the floor, rustling to get up, thinking how I had always seen him moving, standing firm and so strong. Even though my dad was back on his feet, he still needed us to step in and step up more because he needed our help. Our dad was a pastor of a church and had been for forty-plus years. Shortly after he got home, he went back to being Pastor. I remember him laying in the bed, praying with a member who lost a loved one and checking up on a member who was in the hospital the same time he was. Where he did a lot for us and others, we were now doing a lot for him and others. This was tough because we saw how much he needed us, not only to help, but to help him fulfill his duties as a Pastor. This is where that passage of scripture that God put in my face was intensified. When there is a life-changing event that is happening or has happened in our lives, we need that support to lean on, to rest on and that was and still is, Isaiah 55:9-11.

During those challenging times in our lives, we have to start thinking in a selfish manner to get through those times. We have to start asking ourselves, "What did God promise *me*? What did He say?" That is what I did and God saw me through. God promised me that He would always be with me. He said, *"I will never leave you nor forsake you,"* (Hebrews 13:5). It will be done! He also promised that by His stripes, we were healed. His Word says, *"But he was wounded for our transgressions, he was bruised for our iniquities: the chastisement of our peace was upon him; and with his stripes we are healed"* (Isaiah 53:5). It will be done! God say, *"Do not be anxious about anything, but in every situation, by prayer and petition, with thanksgiving, present your requests to God. And the peace of God, which transcends all understanding, will guard your hearts and your minds in Christ Jesus,"* (Philippians 4:6-7). It will be done! *"The Lord is my shepherd, I lack nothing,"* (Psalms 23:1). It will be done! But He said to me, *"My grace is sufficient for you, for my power is made perfect in weakness." Therefore I will boast all the more gladly about my weaknesses, so that Christ's power may rest on me* (2 Corinthians 12:9). It will be done!

Several years later on January 3, 2015, we took my father to the hospital because he was having issues breathing. After many tests, the doctors said Dad needed surgery. My family and I were there with Dad before his surgery, telling him that we loved him and we would see him later. After the surgery, the doctor came out and said, "There were some complications during the surgery. Mr. Moore is a fighter and he needs all of your support." On February 8, 2015 my father passed away.

When I think how God has kept His Word to me, I cry in appreciation and will continue to trust and believe in Him and His Word. When God says it, I believe it and it will be done! When I didn't think I was going to make it and I wanted to give up, I held on to God's Word. I believed God's Word and now when challenges come up, I pray, "Thank you, Lord!" because I know…It Will Be Done!

L'Tarra Moore is the daughter of Pastor George Moore (deceased) and Mrs. Nettie-Lewis Moore. She taught Basic Computers to three to four year olds at Saint Philip Child Development Center for ten years. She is now working on the Marketing Team at Saint Philip A.M.E. Church. She loves to encourage and help people. She is now continuing her education in the technical field, studying Graphic Design, and her new venture is writing.

≫ SHACONDA NELSON ≪

I Belong

I Belong

I can't believe it has been ten years to the date since I heard those words, "Candice, you don't belong here." What I actually heard was, "Candice, you are not in the proper place." I remember it just like it was twenty minutes ago. My mother and I were standing in an elevator in one of the top major design schools in the country. We were going to meet with Mrs. Smith, my entrance counselor. I was wrapped up in a ball of excitement and fear. I had no idea what to expect. All I knew was that I was stepping out on faith and into my dream. I prayed God would guide me during this day and I would start my classes in the spring semester. I graduated from high school the previous year, but I didn't go to college because I didn't know what to go for, at first.

While my thoughts were rolling around in my head and my stomach was turning, my mother looked at me and said, "Candice, you don't belong here."

As soon as those words left her mouth, the elevator dinged; we had come to our stop. I stood there frozen; I couldn't believe what my own mother had said to me. Yes, I had seen every face that walked by us when we entered the building. Yes, I was the opposite of everyone that walked by us that morning. However, inside of me, that was a good thing to me I was different. I didn't apply to that school to fit in, quite the opposite. I wanted to stand out and be the unique individual God created me to be. I was there to get a master's degree and obtain a career in which my heart could be free.

While in the office talking to Mrs. Smith, I took over the conversation. I asked every question that came to mind and spoke with her about my vision for my future. I treated the meeting as if my mother wasn't even in the room. The only time she spoke was when Mrs. Smith asked her if she would be willing to co-sign on a student loan for me. My mother said she was buying a house and no one could run her credit at that time. That was the most crushing moment of my life. I sat there and looked at her in disbelief. My heart was broken and my dreams were shattered. I said my goodbyes to Mrs. Smith and thanked her for her time. I left my hope for a future of my own dreams and wishes right there in Mrs. Smith' office.

I went on with my life, doing what everyone else around me was doing. I worked a job I hated because I needed money, and wasted the rest of my time hanging out with friends. I forgot all about wanting to pursue my dreams of designing anything from office spaces to mansions. Until one day, while getting dressed to go out with friends, as usual, I got the strong desire to find another way to go to school and work my way up to a Master's Degree in Interior Design. The desire was so strong I couldn't shake it. It broke me down into tears; it was something that I had believed I would never have in my life. At that moment, I called up my friends and canceled my plans. I stayed in my room the rest of that evening praying and pouring my heart out to God. I began to search the scriptures on making my request known to God. As well as, "Hope deferred makes the heart sick, but a longing fulfilled is a tree of life". I began to seek God with all my heart because I knew if He was real and if He loved me like His word says He does, he would give me the desires of my heart.

I spent three months doing nothing but going to work and coming home to study God's Word. He was calling me closer to Him and I didn't even know it. As time went on, He began to order my steps. I found a community college to attend in my area that didn't cost that much for an associate's degree. After that, I began to apply for scholarships while working on my bachelor's degree. God was so gracious that He provided multiple ways for me to pay for college without one student loan. His Word does say, *"Owe no man nothing but to love him."* At that time, I didn't understand how exactly we could live and owe no one anything because our culture is so wrapped up in credit. However, God was showing me the way to do it, which was through Him. He provided all I needed to finish my degree.

I searched for a local Interior Designer that would allow me to Intern. I found the sweetest lady named Nancy. She was nice enough to allow me to intern with her around my schedule. I worked, went to school, and interned with Nancy. The most wonderful thing was that Nancy came from that same class of people that my mother said I didn't belong with. I got so acquainted with Nancy that I found myself interacting with almost daily with the same classification of people that I would have been around if I would have gone to the Top National Design College. My mother's words began to resurface. "Candice, you don't belong." I had to challenge those words. I wasn't trying to make my mother out to be wrong as much as I wanted to know why. "Why don't I belong?" God made them just as He made me. Jesus died on the cross for all of our sins. So, why are these even issues floating around in my head? I realized that was it. It was in my head. No one approached me in any disrespectful manner and no one has given me any horrid looks. Maybe this is something that I can choose to live as truth or not. Perhaps, if I focus on the fact that I am not the same race as someone else or if my family isn't in a certain class as someone else's I will only see out of those lenses.

I have come to realize that I can set the tone of whatever conversation I am having and how people perceive me. No, I am not in control of people's thoughts. The truth about that is I couldn't get my own mother to even see how I could be a successful Interior Designer, because of the lenses which she was looking through told her I didn't belong. Well, God said I belong. I belong where ever He places me because He is sovereign and He uses all things for our good and His glory. He uses the good and the evil to conform us to the image of Christ. So, to answer my own wondering question, I decided to see it how God sees it.

Through it all, I accomplished the goal of opening my own Interior Design firm in Chicago, Illinois, which is where I am currently looking out of my window on Wacker Drive. I am amazed at how far I have come. I realize now that it never matters who says you belong if God has called you.

Now I see the reason why I needed to push through and keep going after my dream. God placed it inside of me to go after and achieve it. He purposed me to use what I have achieved to be a blessing to others. I am living my dream. During my spare time, I design the interiors of hundreds of community centers for youth. These are spaces where not only they can come and be safe, but work on their God-given talents while they are still young. If I would have continued to look through the same lens as my mother, I wouldn't have made it this far. I choose not to limit myself to what man thinks of me, but what God has to say about me.

ShaConda Nelson is a Christina Life Coach who desires for everyone to trust God in all they do. Her prayer is that her writing will create an entry point for the Holy Spirit to plant seeds of hope.

⫸ DR. ODUNAYO OBISESAN, CPLC ⫷

Called Out!
By His Grace Only

Called Out!
By His Grace Only

Do you know who you are and whose you are? Do you see adversities and/or challenges as opportunities waiting to be discovered? Do you believe that difficulties sometimes come to prune, strengthen and grow you to become the very best version of yourself?

This story is a snapshot of a piece of my life that speaks to my journey to discovering this in my life.

At age twenty-nine, while going through radiation therapy, I discovered I was pregnant with my second child just months after giving birth to my first! You are probably asking yourself, "Why is a young lady going through radiation therapy?" That is a good question because that was exactly what I was asking myself as I went through this treatment day in and day out until the discovery of my pregnancy.

About two years after gaining admission to college after much adversity, I noticed a growth in my neck. I didn't think much of it for months, but it kept growing and eventually I was referred to a head and neck specialist. He conducted a series of tests, the results of which still left us baffled. I was petrified at this point because this growth could potentially suffocate me. Surgery was recommended and what a surgery it was! I was awake, though couldn't feel any pain. But I remember vividly this intense struggle to dislodge the mass, but that thing refused to come out.

After several hours of cutting and poking around in my neck, the surgeon was finally able to detach this thing. I was so sore by the end of the day; I thought the pain was going to finish the job that the growth started. This was the first of many surgeries. This anomaly would start growing again, sometimes while the most recent surgical wound had not yet healed. Try to imagine trying to complete a very challenging academic program while undergoing multiple surgeries. These abnormal growths strived to take over my life on all fronts.

My parents were frantic. Their healthy, vibrant young daughter almost rendered to a shadow of herself, especially this close to achieving her dream. My prayer warrior mother went to battle, storming the gates of heaven on my behalf. And, our merciful God heard our prayers. I was able to finish my program with honors. The growth however, continued to recur just as soon as it was taken out. These incessant surgeries meant many days of not being able to eat or do much by myself. These were trying times and my faith was truly challenged. Fortunately, my parents were able to help me understand that sometimes these things happen to actually strengthen one's faith. With their prayers and guidance, I was able to adapt to this new normal of several surgeries each year.

During my college years, a fellow student took a fancy to me and pursued me relentlessly, though that was the farthest thing from my mind. But, he truly grew on me. Long story short, we committed to each other. Trying to join my fiancé who was now in the USA, was very challenging since obtaining a visa to the

USA as a young adult in Nigeria was next to impossible. I prayed for God's help constantly and one day, while on the road, I heard very clearly, "I shall never leave you nor forsake you." I looked around, but no one around seemed to be talking to me. I thought that maybe I had imagined it, so I went about my business. But, each time things got really tough and I questioned if our dream was going to be realized, I heard that statement again. I checked my Bible and found a passage that speaks to this in Hebrews 13:5. "This became a companion and as I allowed myself to believe it, I noticed that doors began to open and three years after my fiancé emigrated to the USA, we were reunited.

We got married but of course, the growth was ripe for removal. The surgeon this time around, decided he would aim at a hopefully permanent solution. Then, I got pregnant with my oldest child and just like clockwork, the growth was back. The surgeon sent the removed mass to one of the best oncology hospitals in the country. It took them about a week to get back to us; they weren't sure and asked if it was okay to send it to one of the world-renowned oncologists at the time."

The waiting was excruciating. I prayed as I had never prayed before, asking God for mercy, for Him to spare my life so I could live to take care of my daughter. I confessed every iniquity that came to mind after deep soul searching. I didn't want anything to impact His answer to my cry.

Several evenings later after dinner, my husband suggested we go for a drive. Nothing felt out of the ordinary since we would frequently spend time together driving and exploring new routes whenever he was able to get off work. This evening, I was quite happy and excited he was able to be home before nightfall. I was grateful for the time together. Then, he pulled over and told me the news! Time stopped for a minute. I thought I was drowning, then I heard my heartbeat—loud and overwhelming me with its rhythm. Our daughter slept peacefully in her car seat in the back, oblivious to the devastating news. I still can't tell anyone about the ride home simply because I don't remember one piece of it. We arrived home and it was surreal I was so calm. It was like I was watching a movie of my life and I could see myself going through the motions of getting my daughter ready for bed, feeding her and settling her down for the night. My husband was not sure if I was just in shock or what, but he kept watching me, trying to reassure me…and maybe himself. I assured him I was quite okay and went about my chores.

As I was washing the bottles of my just over one-month-old daughter, it hit me, and an anguished wail escaped my lips. My husband, apparently had been waiting for the reality to hit me and he was able to catch me as I sank to the floor, sobbing uncontrollably. I realized at that time, that there was a strong possibility that I might not live long enough to see my daughter walk or celebrate life's milestones with her. The tears came profusely as I embraced the pain of that possibility becoming reality; of leaving this man I have grown to love so deeply after just a few years of marriage. I couldn't understand it. How could a young woman who just turned twenty-nine be diagnosed with cancer when no one in my family has ever experienced this?

When my tears were spent, I lay in my husband's embrace, our souls knit together in this pain that threatened to swallow us both up. I don't remember how long we stayed that way without moving until our daughter woke up and demanded to be fed.

The following days were a whirlwind of activities— consultations with the medical team and a strong recommendation to wean my daughter off breastfeeding immediately. We waited with bated breath for a definitive verdict from the expert pathologist whether it was benign or otherwise. Finally, my specialist called to tell us that the verdict was in.

I have a name for this growth that had dominated my life for over half a decade! Adenocarcinoma in situ. The growth was deemed non-metastatic, but all the medical folks involved agreed that due to the number of times it had recurred, taking it out alone was not enough. I must undergo radiation therapy to eliminate recurrence and the chance of it turning cancerous.

We met with the radiation oncologist to come up with a care plan, thus began this season of my life more difficult than any I had gone through prior. My week consisted of taking care of my daughter, dropping her off at the babysitter's and heading off to my treatments three times a week. I remember the first time I went in and had my face and neck marked up with different colored inks to delineate the areas of the various radiation doses. I couldn't look at my husband's face and I didn't want him to look at me. I felt so ugly. I cried myself to sleep in spite of my husband's reassurances. To understand radiation therapy is to imagine someone being burnt continuously with a low-grade unseen fire. But within hours, the area turns very scalded as in someone who had just experienced a second- or third-degree burn. And not just on the outside, but inside my mouth, throat and down my esophagus. I wasn't able to eat or swallow for days on end. And, I still had to see to my daughter and go to work.

Most of the time, I wanted to crawl under the first rock I could find, give up and end it all, but for the grace of the Almighty God. This nightmare drove me to my knees constantly more than ever. Due to my heritage, I have always had a relationship with the Lord and I held on tightly to Him during this time. I was led to Psalms 20 and 40 daily; sometimes I recited them several times a day. They were my anchor, along with a song by singer Gloria Estefan, who had been in a near-fatal accident. It was thought that she would not be able to walk again, but she held on to her faith and wrote a heart-pulling song afterward called "Coming Out of the Dark." I listened to it as often as possible, reminding myself that the same God that pulled her through her ordeal can and will do the same for me.

Most of the other patients were in their sixties or older, so I never saw anyone close to my age or even one or two decades older than me. That made me so sad. But, I learned to praise God even while still in the grips of the miry clay.

All glory to God for the man that He gave me to go through this journey with me. He never once wavered, he refused to let me hide or give up, even when I got really mad at him. When I think back, I bless the Lord that my husband supported and encouraged me, but he also didn't allow me to crawl into this ready hold of self-pity and shame. I just couldn't understand. Why me? Pregnant? I was frantic, but isn't it amazing how life plays out sometimes? There I was, focused on enduring each day, but it pleases God to allow a new life into our lives at that time! We were gently encouraged by some of the physicians to explore other options due to the possibility of the baby being harmed already by the radiation. But we decided to trust the God who reminds me often that He will never leave me nor forsake me. I prayed even harder during those long months. And to the glory of my Heavenly Father, my child was born perfectly formed. No one can ever fathom the depth of the relief and thankfulness I experienced.

It has been years and many more things have happened since then. I am grateful the Almighty God spared my life and continues to bless me with excellent health, while I celebrate milestones in the lives of my children and husband. God has truly been faithful through the years.

Dr Odunayo Obisesan is a seasoned healthcare leader who is also a certified life coach. She holds a Doctor of Pharmacy degree and has published in peer-reviewed scientific journals. Dr Odunayo Obisesan has mentored and coached hundreds of young adults and women to accomplish and live their authentic lives; personally and professionally. She has a heart for encouraging and supporting others especially women; accomplishing this through her women's ministry and partnership with other women's ministries.

Dr Odunayo Obisesan recently founded The Young Adult Leadership Forum; a unique organization to help equip our teens and young adults with the needed knowledge and skills to lead themselves successful while seeking to lead others. Her faith in the Almighty God is evident in all that she does. She lives in the USA with her amazing husband and four wonderful children. She is an avid wellness enthusiast who currently contributes Healthy lifestyle articles for publication in a major Nigerian newspaper.

≫ JANET PHILLIPS-CRAWFORD ≪

Finding the Pearl Within

Finding the Pearl Within

Time knows what you do not know. In the fall, leaves on the trees turn beautiful colors before falling to the ground, just as birds know when to fly south to a warmer climate as winter draws near. Squirrels know to store up nuts for the upcoming winter season. In the spring, birds know just when to fly back north to prepare for the mating season. Buds on a flower know the perfect time to bloom into a flower. Nature does have timing. As humans, we have timing as well.

We are created with our own time clock inside of us. No two people are created the same. The timing that is set for me is just that... it is set for me, and yours is set for you. We are created uniquely different, the way we think, and our likes and dislikes.

There are many components of life that help to shape us into the person we are. The people who raised us, the schools we attended, our friends, our family, etc., are all a part of our growth and development.

In regard to you, ask yourself this one question: What is the metaphorical significance of the pearl? What does time have to do with this pearl? What does timing have to do with you? The beauty of the pearl is that it is not just created within one day. It is created over a long period of time. The pearl is created from years of change, test, discomfort, and endurance which in turn yields the iridescent protective coating surrounding a parasite intended to destroy the oyster but instead beautifies it. Such is your life.

How do I know? Let me tell you a story. As a young girl, I often wondered why I was so different from my sisters. They were always the refined and beautiful ones, while I was the uniquely awkward one. More than once I was referred to as "the strange" one or the "eccentric one." Struggling always to fit in, I was always the one that was too tall, too long, or too unconventional looking to be considered average or even common.

Years of consistent external branding caused me to begin to see myself through the eyes of others, invalidating the true intent of my divine nature and dimming the light of truth desperately trying to glow from within.

"You're ugly! Ha Ha! You're not a part of this family!" my sisters would say.

"You could never look like us! Why are you here? Ugh!" they would taunt.

I sought to find the spirit I was given only to believe through the wall of lies that I did not have one. Therefore, I could not find one. Everyone has a pivotal point where a decision must be made…to find your true and authentic self, outside of the lies.

By age thirteen, I performed a self-inventory of the good, the bad, the fearful, the hopeful, the things I knew to be true about me, and the things that I believed could be true about me. During my broken moments sitting upon my bed, I tried to find value in the thirteen years that I had breathed.

Since then, the journey of reflective inventory has been an abundance of turning tides, highs and lows crashing and turning in distinction, but they were mine to ride.

Over the years, I have placed myself into the protective modes, similar to that of an oyster, to protect the areas that caused me pain. Pains that continue to layer and languish over what seems to be eternities but are only a moment.

"Lord! Where is the beauty in this pile of mess?" I asked somewhat expecting an immediate and understood answer.

Sitting on the front steps of my house, three years after my initial inventory, I would receive the soft answer I was looking for. "It is inside of you," the Lord said.

An answer mild but direct was the fuel I needed to continue my search. I knew I needed to search within, to destroy the lies without. As I traveled down life's paths, many layers of protective coating were placed on my beautiful pearl. Coating upon coating rushed to protect my emotions and my heart. The thing that is meant to destroy you will ultimately beautify you, just as the parasite that is meant to kill the pearl gives it its shine.

As I looked for my pearl, I could not find it. I looked deeper and deeper to find just a trace of the pearl but it had no luster. Life happens, and sometimes in the process, it is less than spectacular or beautiful. Knowing this I began to ask questions and search for the authenticity of my pearl. Unlike the oyster, the layers needed to be revealed and not hidden in obscurity. Layer by layer, I began to do the work with tears streaming down my face every lackluster stroke upon lackluster stroke until the hint of shine began to seep through the deepness of my spirit.

By the age of twenty-nine, I was married with one child. I was saved, living for GOD, a Sunday school teacher, a leader in the church, and on the pastor's aid. I believed I had finally gotten it right, but there was still something missing. Since that time I have raised five children in a twenty-five-year marriage where my children's security was more important than my happiness and right to exist in my own family according to my needs for love. A mirror image of the lies I believed only forty years ago in my teens when my sisters questioned my valid place in my family.

At age fifty-five, my children are now married and I have grandchildren, the house was empty and so was I. Discovering the lie that sacrificing my happiness was required for my children's security gave me the strength to move forward into the unknown, because somewhere in the unknown was the truth.

The truth is I am valued. The truth is I am loved. The truth is there is no place for my unhappiness in any relationship where the requirement is love.

When I look at the pearl our creator fashioned, the beauty of the iridescent coating is in the angles, the reflection of light. Every utterance of doubt and dismay gave birth to the rays of beauty and courage that were created for none other than myself and the pearl I was carrying.

Be encouraged! Be strong Be courageous and be brave, everything you need is inside of you. Never stop growing and developing as you explore the inner you. Love who you are and who you were created to be. I have found my pearl.

"You are beautiful and you are unique. You will never fit in because you were created to stand out. Love yourself and shine!" thus sayeth our Creator.

Janet Crawford is a Licensed Cosmetologist, Missionary, and Ordained Minister. Janet has expanded her ministry as far as missionary work in Ghana. Janet is also an Entrepreneur and has owned multiple Beauty salons including but not limited to, Hairs your Glory and Dorcas Closet. The mantra that she lives by is, "All things can be created." Although Standing in God's Grace is Janet's first published endeavor, we look forward to further writings from her gifted hands.

≫ LATANYA SETTLES ≪

My Walk to Health and Wellness

My Walk to Health and Wellness

Growing up, I never had issues with my weight. As a teenager, I rarely worked out. I wasn't an athlete. I was the girl at the games. I wore all black to cover the rolls or appear to be slimmer than I was, but I was doing the same thing as stars like Janet Jackson, and we all wanted to be like Janet Jackson. Seriously, I figured this was normal and I was always going to be a big-boned girl. Like many people, I struggled with yo-yo dieting. I would lose a couple pounds and I was satisfied. Never really knowing how to keep off the weight, I would gain it back. I even starved myself to lose weight or I would resort to the little pink pill, also known as Correctol, which would always give me the relief I wanted in a couple of days. However, after a while, the little pink pill stopped working.

As years went by, I was on a roller coaster ride of losing weight. My weight would range between one hundred thirty and one hundred fifty-five pounds. The fellas liked it and I appeared to have curves. So, I rolled with it.

With my first pregnancy, I gained over seventy pounds, weighing in at a solid two hundred ten pounds. Again, I thought this was normal. Throughout my pregnancy, I ate whatever my heart and baby desired. My favorite was a grilled cheese sandwich. I loved them so much I would eat them twice a day. I never really ate vegetables and drinking water was taboo. I rarely drank more than a glass or two. A week or two before I went in to labor, my boyfriend at the time had taken a weekend trip. When he returned, he said I looked like I had gained twenty pounds and was very swollen and bloated. Can you imagine how I felt hearing that? Again, I assumed this was normal and this was a part of pregnancy. I went into labor, one month early, and I had no idea what was going on. Going through labor was nothing like I had expected. Twelve hours of pushing and puffing, it was exhausting, but whatever the doctors told me to do, I did. Then, the doctor said something I wasn't expecting. I was having complications; the baby was trying to be born breach, so a cesarean was necessary. During my pregnancy, Nana kept telling the doctors something was wrong with this child. She was referring to me. She kept saying, "This child is not this big, and she's bloated beyond recognition," but unfortunately, the doctors weren't listening.

I had a beautiful, healthy, five-pound, eight-ounce baby girl. She was so tiny, but beautiful. All I wanted to do was hold her and love her. Due to the cesarean, I stayed in the hospital for seven days. I was excited about going home, too.

After twenty-four hours of being home, I was having problems breathing. I felt like I was drowning. Every time I would lie down, it felt like my lungs were filling up with water. I was rushed to the emergency room where all the testing began. I was diagnosed with preeclampsia, formerly called toxemia, which is a condition pregnant women develop. It is marked by high blood pressure in women who never experienced high blood pressure. Preeclamptic women will have a high level of protein in their urine and often have swelling in the feet, legs, and hands. This condition usually appears late in pregnancy, generally after the twenty-week mark, although it can occur earlier. If undiagnosed, preeclampsia can lead to eclampsia, a serious condition that can put you and your baby at risk, and in rare cases, cause death. Women with preeclampsia who have seizures are considered to have eclampsia.

Knowing the diagnoses, the doctors tried to bring the situation under control. I was admitted to the hospital. My baby was admitted, too, because she was also having complications. We stayed in the hospital for more than thirty days. It was so critical that every few hours my blood pressure had to be checked because it was uncontrollable at 200/90. I could have had a stroke.

This was so unbelievable. I went from a healthy woman, never having any issues, going to my regular scheduled appointments, to a woman fighting for her life. How could my doctors have not detected this or diagnosed my condition? So many questions, but I had a new baby, who then was diagnosed with yellow jaundice. This was not what I expected. I just wanted to go home and take care of my baby. I wanted to get back to my life after being in the hospital for over thirty days. Finally released, my life was slowly returning to normal. Soon, I was carrying on my daily functions, as if nothing ever happened.

Then, something happened. My fabulous, beautiful, educated grandmother was diagnosed with cancer. How could this be? I watched her battle the fight of her life with cancer. I wondered if there were something different she could have done. As a young woman, who grew up in a Christian home, I know there is a God. We believed on her healing of the cancer. No one ever talk about healthy living. I just thought it was a way of life. Again, never seeing anyone in my family workout or even mention leading a healthy and fit life. My grandmother was healed of cancer, but she passed from breathing complication. So, God does heal, but I wondered what we could have changed in her life that would allow her to live a little longer.

My journey to health and fitness came later in my life, around the age of thirty-six. It was the summer of 2005, after the birth of my second child. I had reached two hundred ten pounds, I was a new wife and mother; this was a drastic change. I felt lost, a little depressed, and desperate and needed a positive way to find myself.

I ran into a friend, who inspired me. She had lost over eighty pounds and was competing in figure competition. At that point, I realized this was attainable and I wanted to transform my body. My eyes were open to fitness.

So began the journey for working on myself. I begin walking five miles a day, rain or shine, five days a week. The struggle was real; I had to unlearn all the wrong things I learned (eating to lose weight, exercise was a must; there were no quick fixes, no fast remedy that would last a lifetime.) The struggle of consistency was real. Initially, my thought was that I might not be able to do this. So many times, I did not want to answer the phone when my friend called or because I was having a bad day. I wanted to quit. I knew I couldn't, though. Eventually, everything began to come together. I didn't see it happening, but it was happening. I had lost the weight. I was down on the scale, but my body was still not quite like my friend's. I was what you would call *skinny fat*. I needed more. Then, I was introduced to weight and resistance training. I was shocked to learn that women could benefit from it, too. I wanted to do whatever it took to stay fit.

I would walk around the gym, speaking the vision into existence. Words are powerful. I wanted to wear cute sweat suits and booty shorts. More than that, I started believing in me. I came to the reality that I am worthy, I am strong, I'm an athlete and I could do all things and I did. Then, I had the vision. I envisioned helping women who may have felt the way I had, needed to find balance in self, and never worked out because maybe they didn't know what to do or maybe felt a little insecure and intimidated about going to the gym. I wanted others to experience the strength and courage I found in fitness in the gym, in lifting weights. I found a way back to loving and working on me. I found a way back to inner strength that the weight was giving me.

I wanted to help women have a better quality of life and who have lost their self due to life's situations, marriage, family, career, life, death, etc. I wanted to help those women find balance again, in themselves and in the higher power that has always been within us.

Now in my eighth year of being a fitness coach, I have had the honor of helping so many women lose weight and begin to find their way back to them. I love what I do, and because I love what I to, I want to make it an infectious movement of getting FitForLife, nutrition, cardio, weights and rest, consistency, dedication to self. *I want women to embrace physical fitness, to have a better quality of life, in every aspect of their wellness life: spiritual, physical, and emotional, financially, socially.*

If there is one thing I could do to encourage another woman to keep going, it is this: first and foremost, you are not alone, that God is with you. No matter how bad it is or how bad it gets, you will make it. Know that you will get tired, but it's okay. Have the courage to keep pressing forward, and have faith in everything you do. Don't judge your circumstance, that's not the real reality.

In everything YOU do, don't forget how to take time for the most important person: YOU. And if you are not taking time to

LOVE you, ask yourself, who will love you? You MUST have patience. No matter how bad it gets, push forward. At the end of pain is success.

YOU must have consistent action. If you fall, get back up. When it hurts, keep on going. Pain is temporary; it may last for a minute, a day, or a year, but it will subside. Dust yourself off. You do have a choice, so make the right choice.

LaTanya Settles is a certified personal trainer, group fitness instructor, and fitness blogger. LaTanya's passion led her to want to uplift, motivate and inspire other women to be FitForLife. AS a fitness competitor, LaTanya has placed in the Top 5 in several National Physique Competitions, including a 1st Place ribbon. Her long-term goal is to become an IFBB professional. An Ohio native, she lives in Columbus with her husband and two daughters. She enjoys motivating others—especially women—to live a fit and healthy lifestyle. FitandFabulousoh@gmail.com

≫ ANGEL TUCKER ≪

Beauty...Redefined

Beauty...Redefined

I grew up in a small town with a population of less than one thousand people, one school, one flashing red light, and one grocery store that closed at six o'clock in the evening, and the most daunting part of it all was that at least ninety-seven percent were made up of people who didn't look like me. Commercials glorified and advertised women with a paler skin tone and hair with a different texture than mine, and that was called beautiful. I thought it was a little amusing after I became an adult and my sisters would laugh at me about never liking [not hating] Cinderella, Snow White, Sleeping Beauty, Belle (from *Beauty and the Beast*), Rapunzel, and just about any other childhood princess you could name. I told my sisters it was because none of them looked like me and the world was brainwashed to believe that if you didn't resemble them you didn't fit the standards of beauty. Sure, all my sisters are women of color and they loved those childhood princesses, and it never bothered them the way it bothered me, and that was just fine.

This is the perfect time to point this out: all things aren't for everybody and all things don't affect everyone the same.

In addition to the princesses, commercials advertising soaps, shampoos, perfumes, clothing, cars, and the things people desired to have didn't have a woman of color connected to it. Can you see why I didn't think that anyone who looked like me was beautiful? I felt no one desired us. We were never connected to anything beautiful. Saturday morning was the only day we would see women of color on television, and that was when *Soul Train* came on. Momma wasn't the biggest fan of those women "twisting" (as she would say), and that bumpety-bump music (her description), so we watched *Soul Train*, but not in peace. [*Gotta love my momma!*]

Honestly, I can't remember anyone treating me differently or unfairly growing up, but seeds were definitely planted in my little mind. I guess if I choose to mention the time I made the cheer team and one of the elders of the school wanted to take cheerleading from me and give it to another popular Caucasian girl. Thank God for a woman by the name of Susan Peters from Houston, Texas, who stood up and said, "That's not happening." I remember how I felt—hopeless and hurt, but I moved on. So I thought.

Around the age of five, I remember experiencing my first moment of being touched inappropriately by a friend. Then it happened again and again, and then with another friend that Mom trusted me to be around. I never told anyone because I felt partly responsible for allowing it to happen, and if I didn't see anything wrong with what happened, why wouldn't I tell someone? Why did I hide instead of making myself be seen?

By the middle of my seventh grade year, our family moved to Fort Worth, Texas. The number of children in my school was more than the entire population of my town I had come from; and the tables were turned—there were more Black children in my school than I had ever seen in my entire life. In my hometown, I was one of two Black girls in a class of three Black students.

Coming from a country town, I was shy with an accent that was totally 'proper', which made me stand out like a sore thumb. If it wasn't bad enough that I didn't have nice clothes to wear, I ended up attending three different middle schools. The first school I had transferred to was pure hell. It started on the bus stop every single morning and then when I got on the bus, one female student, who was fully developed in every way, couldn't wait until I got on the bus to start yanking my ponytails so hard that my neck would hurt. I would sit and look straight ahead and not say a word. By the time I got to school, I had already had the worst day. I don't think I was afraid of her, I was very well disciplined and didn't want to get in trouble and I didn't really know anyone. My sisters attended school together because their ages were much closer. I was all alone. All I ever heard was, "Look at her. She *thank* she cute and talk White." I didn't understand what that meant at all, and the comment about my thinking I was cute was far from the truth. I was a little light-skinned girl with sandy brown hair, brown light freckles and a gap. Truth be told, I never saw myself that way. I always credited the attention I received to being the new girl and being quiet and proper. Things got so bad that finally I didn't want any part of being pretty. Although I didn't feel pretty anyway, I sure wasn't going to allow myself to feel that I was because this pretty stuff was making me be hated.

For my fifteenth birthday, I was molested by two trusted individuals who were never disciplined for what they did to me. *They gave me a card.* I felt like a nothing and nobody, and had to look at them for the next several years, knowing they knew more about how I felt inside than I did. I was tacky, felt unpretty and had been violated...but life went on. I still went to school, told my boyfriend, at the time, that I felt he was all I had. I believe, at that point, somewhere within my mind, I started to create something that allowed me to check out whenever I was in sexual situations, because once they were satisfied it would be all over. The next time I was violated, I was a junior in high school. Our normal routine was to stay after last period athletics and wait for the bus. Instead, another friend of mine, whom I had been quite close with, decided to get assistance from his friend and place me in his truck and drove off. We ended up at his home. I remember being confused because I knew he was a friend, he was cute, but I didn't want him like that. I was friends with him and he was friends with the guy that I liked. I recall getting out of the car and going into his room, and him taking what he wanted. (I had never been in a boy's room before). I didn't think of it as being rape because back then, the only thing I knew about rape was that the guy would beat the girl. I wasn't beaten, so it wasn't rape—I guess. I thought. I dreaded the drive back to the school because all of the teams (freshman, junior varsity and varsity girls and boys) were out there waiting on the bus to take us to the game. That was exactly what one of the girls who was out there needed to see, in order to make things a living hell for me. I was in a relationship with a guy that she had previously dated. So this was news she felt would help her with him. Sad thing was, I had better things to worry about. Women are still that way today. I call it the same game with different players. She fed the rumor wheel, although it wasn't a secret because everyone saw me get dropped off, but my being the person I was, no one said anything. They probably thought about it, but that's about it.

It took several years for these things to come back up to remembrance, and when they did, it was nothing pretty; although, I believe that was the beginning of a series of breakthroughs for me…it was tough. I now had answers to questions that I hadn't quite asked myself.

It was several years later when I finally got a chance to be set free and to forgive myself for the blame of what others had done to me. My friend (my violator) saw me at a night club one night and the first thing he told me was, "I'm sorry. Man, I'm sorry." I knew what he was sorry for already, but I guess I needed him to say it because deep down I still wasn't sure if he saw it the way I saw it. But how did I see it? I never really knew how to categorize what happened. After all, I did get out of the car and walk in the house. Finally he said, "I raped you and I am sorry. I could have been in prison! I've been wanting to say this for years." He just went on and on and I knew he was genuinely sorry. I had never tried to defend myself or my reputation because I grew up believing you should never argue with a man, because they will believe a man and he will make you look bad. I couldn't take that chance. Could I?

Sometimes, I wonder what demons of our past have interfered with our present that is stifling our future. Subconsciously, I believe we, as Black women, are missing out on some of the most beautiful parts of who we are because of the way we see ourselves, or the way others have labeled us or the way we have been told to see ourselves. How do you see yourself? What is beauty to you? Loving you and embracing your true beauty is being okay with everything about you. Flaws in all is what makes you...*you*! I never allow someone to say to me, "You're a beautiful Black woman" or "You're a strong Black woman." It's definitely not negative, but it's telling ourselves or allowing someone else to say we're beautiful *to be* Black, as if that's rare. Words are very powerful. We must learn to use them as food and nourishment to who we are.

I have learned the power of words and how important they are—no matter which way you choose to use them, use them wisely. Whether they are negative or positive, they have power. I didn't use my words, but the other girl used hers, leaving a scar that took a very long time to fade.

I just want to inspire you to never feel bad about where you've been or what you've gone through because what you've gone through will be used (if you allow it) to help someone else. Your past will be the fuel for your future, if you don't give up and allow life to become bitter instead of better. What I experienced, and this is only the tip of the iceberg, has all made me the woman that I am today. I have now become the mouthpiece for those who can't speak up or won't speak for themselves. I have spent the past couple of decades teaching women, teens and girls about their value, self-love and being empowered. My latest project is Mothers Against Prostitution and Solicitation in Schools (MAPS), a 501(c)3 organization (www.mapsinschool.org) that was created to abolish the selling of sex and sexual services in schools. I wonder how many of those girls who are in captivity of human trafficking and participating in prostitution are young ladies with a past and had no one to speak for them? How many didn't know what to say? Who and what stole their words? I am here to give them back and teach them more words.

Today, I speak words of affirmation to remind me that I am fearfully and wonderfully made, above and not beneath. I'm amazing!

※ MARILYNN WALKER ※

My Life in Pieces

My Life in Pieces

I received a call from my sister Brenda who lives in Georgia. I have only known her for a short time. My daddy married her mother, and he had not seen her since she was six months old. Now at fifty years old, she looks like one of my three biological sisters with brown skin, beautiful big brown eyes like Daddy, and a smile that would light up a room.

"Lynn, Daddy is gone. He passed away a few minutes ago," she said.

I had not seen Daddy in a while. He had Alzheimer for over ten years. This hateful illness had made him a different person that didn't even know me, and I was a daddy's girl. He will always be my first love. Daddy was an auto mechanic that worked hard for his family. For a number of years, he owned his own business. Daddy was a tall and handsome man that could have been a movie star. He was called a black Clark Gable.

I flew to McDonald, Georgia, a week before my siblings and mom. We are a large group of three sisters and four brothers. I helped my stepmother and sister with the arrangements and the program. It was a nice program. Daddy looked twenty years younger and peaceful.

Two Weeks Earlier...

I worked as an office manager at one of the oldest law firms in New Jersey. Each day after lunch, my stomach would fill with gas, so I thought it was part of getting older. I would go into my office and close the door, laughing, and saying, "I am taking a real break don't come in." It was painful.

My co-worker said, "I am calling the doctor and making an appointment ASAP," and she did!

I went to the doctor, who sent me to a urologist that was close to work. I was able to schedule an early morning appoint so Jerry, my husband, and I would not be very late for work. Sitting in the office, it was poorly decorated with brown furniture and old green office-looking carpet. It smelled clean, though. The nurse escorted me and my husband to the back quickly. I thought it was going to be a quick appointment. Thirty-five minutes later I hadn't been seen and I was getting crazy. I started getting a little annoyed since no one told us what was going on, but the doctor finally arrived.

"I am so sorry for the wait. I just had to tell a young man around thirty years old he had cancer... The young man was so overwhelmed."

All I could think was, *I hope the doctor doesn't have to tell me that kind of news.*

The next week, I scheduled an early morning appointment for an ultrasound of my stomach at a local center close to home. This place was top notch. The technician, Renee, was very nice. She was a pretty brown-skinned woman, well dressed in a pink nurse's outfit. Renee took her time. She not only viewed the area the doctor requested, but this angle took a picture of the whole stomach. This was going to be a life-changing revelation for me.

About a week or two later, I was back at the doctor's office waiting for the results. He came in very quickly

"I have reviewed your ultrasound and it looks like there may be a mass on your right kidney about the size of a silver dollar. We will need a biopsy to make any kind of conclusion," he said. While he was talking, I kept thinking, *This is just taking too long. Just tell me what's going on.* We scheduled an appointment at a local hospital a couple of days later.

The day of my appointment at the hospital was nice and very cold. Funny thing, I was not even worried. I had an amazing calm about the day. My mom said Jesus gave us peace. For most, that would be irrational. I needed a catscan biopsy where the doctor took a small piece of the tissue and examined it to see what it really was.

While laying wearing only a hospital gown, the procedure started. The doctor took a long needle with what looked like scissors on the end, and snipped a piece of the area. I really did not feel a thing, as the area was numbed before the procedure. All was going well until I heard someone screaming.

"Fire! Fire! Everyone out of the building now! "

"Let me get my clothes," I said.

"No," said the doctor, "we have to get a couple more samples."

There it was again. "Everyone out!"

The doctor said, "We have to take you out now," and I was rolled out of the building on the gurney.

It was one of those cold New Jersey fall mornings. It was so cold, I practically froze wearing a thin hospital gown. Someone got a sheet to cover me. It took over a hour to get the situation under control. I was so done with this look. The doctor said he needed to get a little more, so once we were back inside the hospital, he started again. It took a few minutes, and I was done and headed to work.

Three days later, the doctor's office called for me to come in for the results of my test. Me and my husband went together. I thought it was going to be nothing. I just needed to lose some weight or change my diet.

The look on the doctor's face showed concern. "Well, I have some news about your test…it's positive. I thought, *Positive? For what?* "You have cancer. It's in and around your right kidney. It's very rare and hard to treat. You will need surgery to remove the mass, along with chemo and radiation to fight this cancer since it is so rare. We are not sure what will work at this time."

I thought back to the young man who had received similar news from this same doctor weeks ago. God had already shown me this when I was here before. Sometimes God gives you a small whisper in your ear.

We left the doctor's office and just looked at each other like, as if we both knew what each other was thinking: *Okay, the fight is on.*

I was so calm when I got to work. As I walked to my office, one of the partners approached me about a disgruntled employee who thought I was overworking her, and just was not happy. When I started talking, I fell apart. Tears started running down my face. I really don't know why, but I think at that moment I began to realize what was happening to me… My body was in a fight. I explained to him what was going on and he also started to cry. You see, his wife had just been diagnosed with breast cancer. She was undergoing treatment and it was not going well at this point. This was a hard day for sure.

Next, I told my children and mom. This was hard. We had never expected anything like this in our family, so it was very hard to deal with. Now I know God can give you the right way to handle whatever is going on in your life. My daughter started to pray. I'm not sure how my son was dealing with the thought of losing his mom. I was his only parent. When he was three months old, his dad was killed in a car accident. Life in pieces for another time. My mom started fasting and praying, and kept it up until I had surgery.

I was thinking, *My daddy died so I would not be in heaven alone.* This is how the mind can play tricks on you.

The Day of the Surgery…

"Count backward," the anesthesiologist said as I lay on the operating table in, yet, another cold room. Looking up at the bright, overhead lights, I started counting backward. I felt myself getting sleepy, not really understanding what's going to happen or even if I am going to wake up. Then, everything went dark.

The surgery was over and I wake up to sounds of machines. A short, African-looking man, who looked like a chocolate man in clergy attire, was carrying a Bible and praying for me. *Oh, my God,* I thought, *am I dead because I can't feel anything?* My body was numb at first. Then, I felt the cold tubes and wires all over my body. Monitors were beeping. It was so loud, but yet quiet enough to hear the prayers from the preacherman.

The nurse came over and asked, "How are you feeling?"

"I feel nothing," I said.

"It's fine; you have been in surgery for seven-and-a-half hours. We had to remove one of your kidneys and the vein that was attached. We think we got everything." *Think?*

I did not know Jerry, my mother and my in-laws had been waiting at the hospital the whole time for me. God is so good to put the perfect prayer warriors in your life when you need them.

My mom stayed with me in the hospital for two nights.

"Mama, I want you to go home," I said. "It's cold here and not clean."

She'd talked to my doctor with my husband. I was discharged the next day. Mom treated her forty-three-year-old daughter as if I was her little baby. This was my bonding moment with my mom. After all these years, she was truly my shero.

The ride home was a long one. The incision across my abdomen made laughing hard for me. I needed help for everything, even simple things that are taken for granted—going to the bathroom, taking a shower, fixing a meal. It was truly challenging. The crazy part of the story is I have three sisters and four brothers. I don't think I saw one of them the whole time I was sick. Life in pieces. Family (blood) can be very complicated and self-centered. I am thanking God each and every day for my not holding on to this dark time, and yet opening my eyes.

For nine years, I attended a Methodist AME Church in the town where I live, and I handled the financial records for the church, too. Other than the first lady who visited me because she needed the church's checkbook, the pastor never came to see me and I don't recall any of the church members coming to visit me. I did not think much of it at the time. I was focused on getting well for my children and husband. This was when I knew you had to have God in you, because people don't always do what says the Lord.

Sometimes it is when you are flat on your back that the devil truly gets busy. My daughter, Kalimah, never had any issues at school. One day, she had gotten into a fight that had gotten out of control. The fight was racially motivated. It truly got out of control. It became racial. This was followed by a horrible racial comment on the school's website. She and the girl were suspended from school. This was just one more thing added to the stress of fighting cancer. Through it all, we kept giving God the praise and the worship. This mess would not change God's plan for our home.

Time flew by quickly. I watched all the trash TV shows. Jerry Springer became the show I would watch all day, every day. Since this was the dead of winter, my mom and Aunt Margaret, who was Jerry's aunt and was around eighty-five years young, would come over most days to help me out. I will love them forever... my angels.

When I returned to the surgeon, who by the way was very good, I had no visible scar, which was nice. Although, it wasn't like I was going to wear a bikini anytime soon.

For two months, I worked from home a couple days before I returned to the office only to learn the office was closing a couple months later. Now, I was out of work. But, the funny thing was I did not go crazy. I just got another job the following week before the hammer even got next to the desk. The partners were like: "Marilynn, we are not ready for you to leave." I don't wait for things to happen. When God says move, I move. Besides, I still had radiation and chemo treatments to do. There was no time to waste on a place that was not sure what was happening or how things were going to pan out.

My God moment was a place where I had worked for fifteen years allowed me stay on the insurance and let me work part-time until I found something I loved, and I did. LOOK AT GOD!

I received a call from my doctor stating my last CAT scan looked great. Now I needed to make an appointment to see the gynecologist. Within a couple days, I had the ultrasound and papsmear. The results came back quickly. The cancer had found its way into my uterus. I needed a total hysterectomy to stop the cancer from spreading. The surgery was booked. It was only thirty days from my last surgery and the doctor was not sure if it was good to do this so quickly. God was speaking to me: *Don't wait, do this now*, and so I did.

I truly did not know if I wanted to have more children. I was forty-three and that ship had sailed. I got prepared for surgery. Lights out again. This time, I went to a nicer hospital in New Jersey thinking the service would be great. I noticed while waiting for my turn…yes, my turn. It must have been eighteen people waiting for surgery that day…I was taken into a room of bright lights. I was told to start counting backward. That's all I remember.

When I woke up, there was no little preacher, just machines and Jerry and Mom waiting for me to come back to my room. I was asleep most of the day. The next day, I was told to get up and walk around. I really felt a lot of pain. I thought it was normal. On day three, I went home, feeling the worst pain, but the doctor said "Go home, you will feel better soon." On day four, I was back in the hospital for a week. A staph infection. This was a lesson—when you don't feel right, say something and don't take *no* from anyone.

Now the fight began. I needed to have radiation for thirty days. Around the tenth treatment, my stomach was getting burned. It was a little painful, but truly not that bad. I remember laying on the table asking for my angel to guide the hands of the radiologist. Before my first surgery, a women said to me, "God has angels that we can call on," so I always do.

Chemotherapy was crazy! The doctor said I only needed five treatments. I thought, *That isn't so much*, after I had seen people who needed to have more. I was glad that was all I needed. After the second treatment, my hair started to fall out. At the time, I had let it grow long. I don't use chemicals in my hair. I have always been a bit of a heath nut. Some of the other side effects— fingernails and toenails turned black, tongue turned very dark, my ears got very dark, my skin was dry, and some hair fell out that, to this day, never grew back. Praise God I got a little sick, but nothing like you see in the movies or on television. The months went by fast.

Today it's been thirteen years of freedom from one of the rarest cancers called Leiomyosarcoma, also referred to as LMS, a malignant smooth muscle tumor. I am doing great. I love life each day to the fullest, drinking in each day, moment by moment. Finally, I am in love with me. Don't live with limits NEVER AGAIN.

God bless you all and thanks for reading my story.

Marilyn Walker is the owner of THE BELL TOUCH, a bookkeeping and office management consulting service in New Jersey. She also enjoys turning her living room into a photo studio and event planning. Her motto is "Transforming ordinary into extraordinary events is what we do. " Marilynn has a heart for helping business owners organize their finances and document management so the da- to-day operation can be stress free. In her free time, she works as a Trustee in her church (Gethsemane Baptist Church, Newark, NJ) , President of their Missionary Ministry, and recently spear-headed the opening of the Sunday Nursery for newborns to four year olds. Three times a week you can find Marilynn in the gym working out her health regiment. Her life is a balance of exercise, prayer, sensible eating and finding a passion that gets you out of bed in the morning. Be Fearless. Be you.